# NONSENSE ON STILTS

"The editors have marshalled a good cross section of viewpoints to address the question: Is the way we are using human rights devaluing the currency? Opinionated but well informed, these academics, lawyers, and politicians have wrestled directly with contemporary Australian challenges. The book is balanced by two editors with contrasting views and a variety of respondents with opposing views on institutions like the Australian Human Rights Commission and the Parliament's Joint Committee on Human Rights. All agree that the gravest danger to human rights is the constraint placed on discourse and debate about the conditions under which people can participate in shaping the kind of society in which they live. This book is a great primer for that discourse and debate, particularly in relation to issues which are deemed politically correct. It will be a significant contribution to the perennial Australian discussion about the desirability of a national Human Rights Act or how best to enhance public conversation, law, and policymaking without one."

FRANK BRENNAN SJ AO
Chair of the 2009 National Human Rights Consultation

"Nonsense on Stilts is a provocative series of essays that question what human rights mean in the Australian political, academic, and legal landscapes of 2019. The essays bring together a range of perspectives about the nature of human rights and their relevance to Australia. Collectively, the authors highlight Australia's immaturity, compared to other nations, with respect to understanding human rights and developing appropriate human rights policies, laws, and institutions."

KATE EASTMAN SC
2019 Human Rights Awards finalist

"Australia's system of human rights is in deep trouble. Real rights, such as freedom of speech and religion, are under attack in ways that have become an international embarrassment. Yet any attempt to rescue human rights in this country requires a clear understanding of what is, and is not, a real right. This book will disrupt the mindset that has produced a rights infrastructure that is distorted, expensive and frequently out of step with community values. Those responsible for striking the balance between conflicting rights will find this book invaluable. It challenges the certainties that have left human rights protection in a confused and vulnerable state."

CHRIS MERRITT
Legal affairs editor at The Australian

# THE KAPUNDA PRESS

an imprint of Connor Court Publishing
in association with the PM Glynn Institute

Series editor:
*Damien Freeman*
PM Glynn Institute
Australian Catholic University

### CHALICE OF LIBERTY
PROTECTING RELIGIOUS FREEDOM IN AUSTRALIA
*Frank Brennan – M. A. Casey – Greg Craven*
(2018)

### TODAY'S TYRANTS
RESPONDING TO DYSON HEYDON
*Frank Brennan – Anne Henderson – Paul Kelly – M. A. Casey – Peter Kurti
M. J. Crennan – Hayden Ramsay – Shireen Morris – Michael Ondaatje
Sandra Lynch – Catherine Renshaw*
(2018)

### FEDERATION'S MAN OF LETTERS
PATRICK MCMAHON GLYNN
*Anne Henderson – John Fahey – Anne Twomey – Peter Boyce
Suzanne D. Rutland – Patrick Mullins*
(2019)

### STORY OF OUR COUNTRY
LABOR'S VISION FOR AUSTRALIA
*Adrian Pabst*
(2019)

Forthcoming:

### THE MARKET'S MORALS
RESPONDING TO JESSE NORMAN
*Tania Aspland – Gregory Melleuish – Amanda Walsh – Adrian Pabst
Michael Easson – Parnell McGuinness – David Corbett – Cris Abbu – Tom Switzer
Marc Stears – Leanne Smith – M. A. Casey*
(2019)

# Nonsense on Stilts

## Rescuing human rights in Australia

Damien Freeman
Catherine Renshaw

Copyright © 2019 as a collection, Damien Freeman; individual chapters, the contributors.

Published by Connor Court Publishing under the imprint of The Kapunda Press. The Kapunda Press is an imprint of Connor Court Publishing in association with the PM Glynn Institute, Australian Catholic University.

ALL RIGHTS RESERVED. This book contains material protected under International and Federal Copyright Laws and Treaties. Any unauthorised reprint or use of this material is prohibited. No part of this book may be reproduced or transmitted in any form or by any means, electronic or mechanical, including photocopying, recording, or by any information storage and retrieval system without express written permission from the publisher.

CONNOR COURT PUBLISHING PTY LTD
PO Box 7257
Redland Bay QLD 4165
sales@connorcourt.com
www.connorcourtpublishing.com.au

Cover image: Karel (Karl) Palda, amber glass duck decanter, c.1930 – 1940. Australian Catholic University Art Collection.

ISBN: 9781925826685 (pbk.)

Cover design by Ian James

Printed in Australia

"Natural rights is simple nonsense: natural and imprescriptible rights, rhetorical nonsense—nonsense upon stilts."

Jeremy Bentham

# Contents

Prologue: the end of human rights? — ix
*M. A. Casey*

Introduction: rights, nonsense and the commentariat — 1
*Damien Freeman and Catherine Renshaw*

## Two approaches to rescuing human rights in Australia

In the long grass — 19
*Damien Freeman*

Where the light gets in — 41
*Catherine Renshaw*

## Responding to Damien Freeman and Catherine Renshaw

1. The use and usefulness of human rights in our parliament — 61
*Terri Butler*

2. A constant conversation — 73
*Tim Wilson*

3. Disagreeing about rights and interests — 83
*Emma Dawson*

4. Our common lives — 91
*Nicholas Aroney*

5. Splitting our differences — 97
*Jennifer Cook*

6. Human rights versus citizenship — 109
*Bryan S. Turner*

Contributors — 122
Notes — 123
Index — 135

# Prologue: the end of human rights?

M. A. Casey

The future of human rights was identified as an area of particular focus for the PM Glynn Institute when it was established as the public policy think-tank of Australian Catholic University in 2016.

The intention was not so much to focus on specific human rights issues alone—a crowded field where plenty of good work is already being done. Instead, the major purpose of the Institute's human rights work stream is to consider a larger question: whether the uses of human rights in public debate and how they are approached and applied in some areas raise questions about the coherence and longer-term sustainability of human rights in democratic societies. The short form of this question might be: Is the way we are using human rights devaluing the currency?

This question arises from a conviction about the fundamental importance of human rights, not only in shaping the character of free societies, but in protecting the lives, integrity, and freedom of all individuals, irrespective of the society in which they live. It carries with it an assumption that human rights belong to everyone, and anything which detracts from this strikes directly at the credibility of human rights as a shared frame of justice. If there are in fact trends which foster an apprehension that human rights only belong to some people and not others, or only to privileged societies or classes, or that they are largely the preserve of particular political cohorts who can use them against the rights of others to advance their own vision of justice, we need to take this seriously and correct course. Human rights limited and re-defined in this way are no longer *human* rights.

Alternatively, if none of this is the case it would be good to have concerns like these resolved and the facts clearly established. If there are problems, however, they should be given serious attention and addressed. Clarifying this question is the main purpose of the Institute's work stream, "The End of Human Rights?". It is an important task, because complacency about the authority and general acceptance of human rights, especially in democratic societies, is dangerous. It makes it easy to overlook indications of disengagement with human rights; to dismiss signs of disenchantment as mere prejudice; and to assume that a commitment to human rights is a measure of justice which can never err.

To consider the end of human rights as a question is not to prejudge these matters. A question, after all, is not an answer. Nor is it an expression of pessimism; a surrender to apocalyptic thinking or prophecies of doom. It is simply to acknowledge that the period which commenced after World War II and saw the birth and development of modern human rights, with all the advances this brought for different groups of people living under legal and social barriers in the West, has now ended. Hannah Arendt once observed that "the end of a period or a tradition or a whole civilisation is a new beginning for those who are alive".[1] So the task is not to lament the end but to try to understand what has begun.

The classical period of human rights in the post-war decades was underwritten by a high but abstract belief in a shared humanity and the possibility of a life in common. Its most glorious achievement was to make the abstract real (or more real) by expanding the more narrowly-drawn boundaries of the time around ideas of a shared humanity and by creating a more capacious sense of a life in common in different societies. The most conspicuous example in the Western world is the repudiation of racism as a legitimate way of thinking about human life and social order.

However, this success has contributed to the rise of other forms of abstraction which have now begun to contradict this achievement—even as more and more legal and social barriers continue to fall for further classes of people previously constrained by them, and the triumph of human rights seems more secure and sweeping than ever before. Abstractions can be helpful, but people do not live in the abstract. Human beings are individual and particular, with identities, commitments, and relationships utterly personal to them. In highlighting this reality, most especially for classes of people excluded from more restricted or 'local' understandings of a shared humanity and a life in common, human rights has played an indispensable part in broadening and deepening these understandings. It has also set a train of logic running in the opposite direction by making identity and particularity themselves forms of abstraction.

It seems that bringing the particular and the individual to the fore, with all the benefits this has brought in terms of agency and recognition for previously marginalised groups, has been shadowed by the receding of a compelling idea of a shared humanity and a life in common. In part, the causes of this lie in the developments accompanying the growing size and complexity of modern societies, reinforced by the ease with which people can separate themselves from each other, either as individuals or as communities. The broader context is added to by various lines of scientific and scholarly enquiry which have raised questions not just about whether there is any shared human essence or nature across cultures and time, but also about what it means to be human and what shapes human thinking and values. The logic of human rights has fed into this as well. Paradoxically, an enlarged appreciation of the complex particularities of different individuals, communities, and societies has helped to make the idea of a common humanity more elusive.

Human rights, at least in the form understood philosophically as inhering in each human being simply by virtue of being human, depends absolutely on some concept of a shared humanity. Any shift towards a position which either implicitly or explicitly casts doubt on the possibility of shared humanity would seem to be fatal to the very notion of *human* rights (as opposed to various legal, civil, or political rights, which are purely within the gift of the state, or otherwise arise from custom and culture). It would in effect return us to the default of the human condition, where the compass of shared humanity, and any rights it might accord, are drawn primarily around the tribe or clan to which you belong, with those outside these closed circles being something very much other.

These points remind us that human rights obviously have important conceptual dimensions, going to questions around their origin, their source and scope, and the ultimate foundation of their legitimacy or authority. A consensus on these conceptual dimensions has never been achieved. My own sense, as an interested outsider, is that at least some of these questions have been tacitly abandoned, with attention focussed much more on the practical outcomes for suffering people which human rights still produces so powerfully. This preference is completely understandable. A solution to the conceptual problems underlying human rights will probably always evade us. Against this, human rights have a very practical purpose, first, in trying to ensure that the fundamental conditions for a life which can properly be called human are secured and available for all people; and secondly, by fostering the possibilities for human flourishing beyond basic security of existence and personal freedom.

In the absence of both concord about the source and authority of human rights and comity in the sciences and humanities about something like a shared human nature, the practical imperatives that human rights are intended to serve direct our energy towards human needs and aspirations, as a minimal and more or less uncontested given about the human condition from which we can work. For these practical purposes that have become the main concern of human rights, what it means to be human is reduced to the will. We are creatures that need things and want things, and human rights help us to secure certain classes of needs and wants which are most critical to life and flourishing. It is a concept of the human which can be filled out in various interesting ways, but at its foundation it remains very slender. To the extent that this thin concept of a shared humanity also serves, in effect, as the foundation of human rights, it provides only a loose footing at best. The slippage which comes with this explains some of the problems which raise the question about the end of human rights.

The distinction between needs and wants can be expressed more completely as a distinction between goods and claims. Human goods comprise all that is needed to live securely in freedom and dignity. Human claims go to what is sought to enhance or enrich an individual's life. It is a distinction which is of course subject to imprecision and ambivalence. What is needed to live as a human being is very much wanted when it is absent; and what we want in pursuit of a more fulfilling and more meaningful life can often be felt as a most urgent need. That which is needed is most certainly owed to us, but that which is wanted may also be seen as something certainly owed. Perhaps the distinction can be thought of as being between the necessary preconditions to live as a human being—security of the means of life, freedom from slavery, torture and domination, freedom of thought and belief, freedom to work and hold property, etc; and the contingent additions for a human life with maximised individual choices—some flashpoint examples being access to abortion or euthanasia, to reproductive technology and surrogacy, recognition for different relationships as forms of marriage, freedom to seek gender reassignment, to be protected from offence or disparagement, etc.

To describe the second category of requirements as contingent is not to deny the importance they may have for particular individuals. They may indeed be felt to be absolute requirements. Unlike absolute requirements, however, this second category of requirements can more frequently entail some significant level of impingement on others—and even harm—which raises further questions of justice. They are contingent not only because people may disagree over whether they are absolutely required to live as a human being, in the same way that security of the means of life and freedom from slavery and subordination are, but also because they inevitably involve negotiation, or more usually conflict, with the rights of others. Complicating the picture further, arguments intended to advance recognition of these contingent requirements as rights tend strongly to cast them as absolute requirements and as fundamental rights. This is where the question of the end of human rights arises most acutely: because of the conflicts it tends to generate, does our changing understanding of human rights, and particularly what constitutes a fundamental right, make the concept of human rights more coherent and compelling, or more fragmented and questionable?

The problem here is not the growing number of rights in itself, or the expansion of understanding about what older rights might entail. Part of the work of human rights is to deepen our appreciation of the humanity of the neglected or disadvantaged groups among us, and, to the extent that it serves this purpose, the expansion and growth of rights is to be expected and welcomed. The key question is how it all comes together. Above all, this is a question about whether new rights and new understandings of rights are broadly consistent with what human rights are about, or in fact to some greater or lesser extent contradictory with what human rights are about. These issues are inherently complex. The expansion of human rights to new areas will always be contested, and part of the noise confusing the matter comes from the way human rights are often invoked in political argument to privilege particular positions against others, although it is usually not difficult to sift out these claims from genuine human rights issues. At the same time, however, human rights which were once seen as being at the very essence of democracy, such as freedom of religion and belief, freedom of speech, and freedom of association, are called into question and demoted to distant second-order matters, particularly when they come up against certain issues concerning life and death, sexuality and identity, and discrimination and equality. Some of the clearest fault lines can be found in areas such as freedom of conscience and the right to conscientious objection, particularly in healthcare.

For example, in June 2016, a Consensus Statement on Conscientious Objection in Healthcare was developed by a group of bioethicists meeting at the Brocher Foundation in Switzerland.[2] The statement describes the rights that medical practitioners still have in many places to conscientiously object to participating in procedures such as abortion or "medical assistance in dying" as "indefensible". It calls for conscientious objections in healthcare to be tested before tribunals for sincerity and "reasonability" and for conscientious objectors to "be required to compensate society and the health system for their failure to fulfil their professional obligations". It also calls for medical students to learn "how to perform basic medical procedures they consider to be morally wrong", because they should be required to perform these procedures in "emergency situations". Whatever we might make of this suggested approach, it is a long way from the esteem accorded freedom of conscience in the decades following World War II and into the Vietnam War, when it was invoked to protect the rights of those who conscientiously objected to military service, and was regarded in many ways as the most emblematic of human rights.

Another example concerns the narrowing down of the category of human beings who are bearers of rights. In 2012, an article published in the *Journal of Medical Ethics* attracted attention for arguing that it is permissible, even socially desirable, to make infanticide available for a wide range of social and environmental reasons.[3] It claimed that personhood is not intrinsic to human infants but something accorded to them by others: "Individuals who are not in the condition of attributing any value to their own existence are not persons. Merely being human is not in itself a reason for ascribing someone a right to life".[4] In the absence of being accepted as a person by someone else, a human infant is a "non-person" with "no moral rights to life", and non-persons are not harmed by a decision to end their lives.[5] The authors of this article attempt to confine its implications to infants and new-borns but it is unclear that its logic will be constrained in this way. If the first premise is that "individuals who are not in the condition of attributing any value to their own existence are not persons", then there are many other categories of non-persons which could be identified among the mentally ill, the drug-afflicted, those who have suffered brain injuries, those with certain advanced neurological conditions, and even perhaps those who have simply been abandoned to loneliness and depression. It is a line of reasoning which raises grave concerns for the concept of inherent and inviolable human dignity, but also for human rights. Human rights become something other than human rights if they do not apply universally. Dividing human beings between persons and non-persons does not preserve this requirement, as some may like to think, but fatally undermines it.

Human rights are meant to protect human life and flourishing. Rights which contradict this purpose pose a problem. Which rights these might be, however, depends on how we understand the purpose. Ideas of human flourishing, and even what constitutes a life that is properly called human, have multiplied since the middle of the twentieth century and point in very different directions. Unsurprisingly, the understanding of life and flourishing that we work from determines which rights appear problematic. Older understandings would see a right to abortion or a right to euthanasia, for example, as rights that contradict the purpose of human rights. Much newer understandings see freedom of religion and freedom of speech, for example, as rights contradicting the protection of life and flourishing. Of course, if human rights are not in fact about protecting human life and flourishing, but more a matter of managing competing interests in a community, or about what the law grants or permits at any given time, none of this is a problem. The meaning of rights simply changes with changing values. Assuming that human rights entails a higher ambition, however, we find ourselves in a cluttered and confusing landscape. In attempting to navigate a way forward, it may help to re-orient ourselves from some reliable bearings.

The first is the inescapable reality of human weakness. It has always been possible for anyone with a modicum of power or an advantage over another to claim that they are entitled—that they have a right—to do as they want. The revolutionary nature of human rights lies in the way it overthrows this logic to focus primarily on the rights of the powerless, and what the strong owe to them simply by virtue of a shared humanity. No human being escapes the experience of weakness, despite the massive and complex structures of denial we have built against it, and whatever we might take the protection of human life and flourishing to mean, it must mean the protection of all of us when we are weak. Priority has to be accorded to the weakest; those who know only powerlessness, who have been deprived of the agency to articulate valid rights claims and rendered voiceless by their vulnerability, arising either from their personal circumstances or from structures of dependence or subordination maintained against them by others.

The second bearing for re-orienting ourselves is friendship. It is one thing—no mean thing—to acknowledge obligations to each other from our shared humanity. The high idealism of human rights, however, suggests going beyond this. The first article of the Universal Declaration of Human Rights, using the language of the time, states that all human beings "should act towards one another in a spirit of brotherhood". Friendship is perhaps the better term for our situation today, particularly in a context where politics is increasingly practised on the basis of enmity. This friendship has its basis in being "born free and equal in dignity and rights" and "endowed with reason and conscience". A shared human nature, it seems, can extend to something more than goods and claims, needs and wants, the subject who wills. In addition to freedom and equality, it also comprises rationality and a relationship to the truth. The invocation of "a spirit of brotherhood" or friendship calls attention to how Western societies balance autonomy and solidarity; individual freedom and self-determination, and respect for the network of relationships and obligations in which individuals are enmeshed, both with those most immediately around them and with the larger community. On the face of it at least, uses of human rights which result in certain rights being read down or heavily qualified, so that others may be prioritised, suggests that the balance between the autonomy and solidarity is tilted in autonomy's favour. Friendship requires a practice of human rights which holds autonomy and solidarity together in a better, more humane, balance.

The idea of autonomy is often dramatised by opposing it to various ideas of order and control, and by celebrating it as a means of expanding the scope of individual self-determination against systems of power. There is, of course, much truth in this representation, particularly when it comes to defending the rights of vulnerable people against government and unjust or tyrannical systems of commerce and labour. Autonomy is also heroised against moral constraints on personal freedom, and celebrated for the way it enables individuals to push out the boundaries and test what freedom can encompass. But solidarity is not a synonym for order, control, and moralised constraint. When autonomy is opposed to solidarity in Western countries, it is in effect asserted against those things intended to foster a life in common where all can flourish—in particular, the various obligations we have for the well-being of those around us. Every balance limits how much of something can be placed in the scales, and in this sense solidarity is a limiting factor on autonomy. It is an unusual limiting factor, however, because solidarity is not opposed to freedom. Freedom is an essential element of a life in common which enables people to flourish, and for this reason solidarity seeks to foster and enlarge it, within an enlarging compass of friendship. This task inevitably entails keeping forces which pull in opposite directions in tension; the testing and expansion of freedom with holding things together for the good of all. It is not clear at all that autonomy, as it is currently understood and practised, can co-exist with solidarity, except insofar as solidarity is relegated effectively to a second-order priority. A recalibration becomes possible when we recognise that freedom and solidarity go together.

We continue to rely on human rights to defend people when the absolute requirements of human existence are denied to them, and in this context the language and ideas of human rights retain immense and valuable power. Are we compromising the force of the moral claims that human rights makes in these situations by elevating more contingent requirements, often asserted against the rights of others, to the same level? The question about the end of human rights, therefore, comes down to whether the default is set to an assertion of the needs and requirements of the individual against other people, or to a means of meeting individual needs and requirements in solidarity with other people. The answer to this question is still open, and serves as an invitation to try to trace out honestly the possible directions in which the logic currently in play may take us.[6]

# Introduction: rights, nonsense and the commentariat

Damien Freeman and Catherine Renshaw

It is hardly surprising that the French Revolution should have excited the attention of the English commentariat in 1789 as much as claims about human rights and their abuse excite the Australian commentariat today.

Perhaps the most famous reaction in England was that of Edmund Burke, an Anglo-Irish politician and theorist, who almost immediately penned his influential *Reflections on the Revolution in France*. Published in 1790, it is the work of a man who had a reputation as a reformer, but who was shocked by the kind of change that the French Revolution involved. He correctly predicted that the revolution would lead to the Reign of Terror, and he was spurred on to develop his account of modern conservatism, which supports tradition, gradual change, and deference to authority, in contrast to the French Revolution's programme of change based on abstract principles, radical change, and popular agency.

The following year, Thomas Paine, the English radical who emigrated and became an American revolutionary, responded to Burke's critique of the French Revolution with his *Rights of Man*, published in 1791. He defends the revolution against Burke's critique, and, in doing so, he explains why he takes exception to Burke's attitude. He accuses Burke of lacking compassion for those who suffered in the Bastille and of being unaffected by the reality of the distress experienced by ordinary Frenchmen under the Ancien Régime.

Paine waxes lyrical about the suffering, his sympathy for the distress caused by injustice, and the need to do something to make the world a better place once one feels that the natural dignity of man has been compromised by any government anywhere. For him, 1789 is not a moment at which order gives way to chaos, but a moment at which a declaration emerges championing the natural rights which decent people *feel* cannot be taken away from anyone by an unjust government. It is in such a response to the French Revolution that the modern human rights movement lies.

Like Paine, Jeremy Bentham may well have sympathized with the distress that motivated the French Revolution and the need to give expression to the feeling of disgust at how human beings had been violated in a way that they should not be in future. Where Bentham differs most profoundly from Paine, however, is in his inability to accept that the revolution's Declaration of the Rights of Man and the Citizen was an appropriate way to give expression to it. His contribution to discussion about the declaration seems to have been written around 1796, but was not published until 1816, and in French, under the title, *Sophismes anarchiques*. It was not published in English until 1834, two years after Bentham's death, and then with the title translated as *Anarchical Fallacies*. His preferred title for the work was, however, *Nonsense on Stilts*.

The nonsense to which Bentham took exception was the Declaration of the Rights of Man and the Citizen, published by the National Assembly on 27 August 1789. This declaration was nonsense, he believed, because it purported to articulate a set of rights in a way that depended upon natural law. Bentham then took it upon himself to offer one of the most influential critiques of natural law, with the intention of showing that any such declaration that depended upon natural law was fundamentally misguided.

In *Nonsense on Stilts*, Bentham goes through the declaration, article by article, analysing each in turn. The gist of his analysis is that the declaration's assertions are all either false, nonsense (incapable of being either true or false), or so uncertain in their meaning that it is not possible to say whether they are true or false. Bentham is not opposed to the idea that the law should confer certain rights on all people. He utterly rejects the claim, however, that one can prove through reason alone that people have rights in virtue of being human, and that the law must recognise those rights. This is to say that he rejects the theory of natural law.

Bentham's critique remains of relevance to contemporary debates for the argument it makes against natural law, but also as a critique of human rights, whether or not it is founded in natural law. Human rights have assumed an ever-increasing moral and political significance since World War II, and so it is important to consider whether they are simply nonsense on stilts, and, if not, why they do not fall foul of Bentham's critique of the Declaration of the Rights of Man and the Citizen.

Natural law is a philosophical theory about the relationship between law, morality, the cosmos, and human nature. It makes the claim that we can deduce through reason or empirical observation facts about the world that establish moral principles that are the basis for any system of human law. It follows that human lawmakers do not *make* the law. Rather, they implement the law that exists independently of them. The natural law might be understood as God's intention for creation, as Saint Thomas Aquinas held; but it might also be understood as moral precepts that are binding on all rational beings simply in virtue of their rationality, as Immanuel Kant held.

Natural law is a tempting foundation for human rights. If it can be established that there are certain rights that must be accorded to human beings in virtue of their human nature, then the basis of human rights is given. The problem is that it is difficult to establish through reason or empirical observation that human beings in fact have a nature that *requires* them to be treated in a particular way.

This goes to the heart of Bentham's objection to declarations of human rights. Such declarations might be understood as being aspirational—giving form to our ambitions for how we would like to see human beings treated. But these declarations clearly purport to go further than that. They claim to recite not merely how human beings *ought* to be treated, but how they *must* be treated. They lay claim to a code of conduct to which any government *must* adhere, rather than merely a code to which any government *ought* to adhere. The difficulty with making this larger claim is that it is not possible, as a matter of reason, to demonstrate why any government must adhere to this code, as opposed to merely appealing to governments to adhere to it.

If one does not accept the claims of natural law, then it is not possible to find a foundation for human rights in metaphysics or rationality. That is not to say that it is impossible to find a foundation. One might attempt to found human rights in sentiment, for example. If human rights depends on sentiment, however, it cannot have the same sure foundations that it has if it is anchored in metaphysics or rationality. It is not open to any rational being to deny human rights that are derived from the nature of the universe or from rationality itself. It is open to a person to deny human rights that are anchored in sentiment, if that person happens not to share that particular sentiment. The challenge then is to get people to feel disposed towards each other in a way that imposes an obligation upon them to respect one another's human rights.

However one unravels the connections between human rights, law, and ethics, it is important to acknowledge that claims about human rights can be claims about how states should treat human beings, a matter for ethics and political thought. They can also form a distinct set of claims about what states can and cannot do to human beings within their jurisdiction—a matter for law. In the domain of politics, we are largely concerned with human rights as claims about how people ought to be treated, whereas in the domain of law, we are concerned with how people can or cannot be treated.

As a political claim about how people should be treated, human rights seek to affirm the dignity of the human being. If human beings have a special value—perhaps, because they are made in the image of God—perhaps, because they are rational beings—then it follows that there is a reason why this special value should be respected. This value we might call human dignity. Human rights is then one means of affirming human dignity; it seeks to call out conduct that undermines human dignity.

There is a world of difference, however, between affirming human dignity and protecting human dignity. To protect human dignity is to prevent conduct that undermines human dignity. When human rights becomes a claim about protecting—rather than merely affirming—human dignity, it has become a matter of law. This might be a matter of preventing one human being from undermining the dignity of another human being. It might also be a matter of preventing the government of a state from undermining the dignity of human beings within the jurisdiction of that state. If one does not subscribe to some form of natural law, then it is not obvious how claims about affirming human dignity can be turned into claims about protecting human dignity. In other words, it is not obvious how moral claims about human rights can be turned into legal claims that are enforceable in courts of law.

Concern about the atrocities committed by Germany during World War II, coupled with the more general desire to avoid resolving international disagreements through warfare, meant that the establishment of the United Nations, as a replacement for the League of Nations, was motived not only by the imperative of providing a forum for resolving international disputes through diplomacy, but also for the establishment of international organisations that could monitor human rights issues within member states.

Australia was one of the founding member states of the United Nations, and participated in the meeting held in San Francisco on 25 June 1945 at which the Charter of the United Nations was adopted. The Charter came into force on 24 October 1945, following ratification by Russia. The purpose of establishing the United Nations was to maintain international peace; to develop friendly relations among nations, based on equality and self-determination of all nations; and to achieve international cooperation in solving international problems. The Charter provides for the General Assembly, consisting of representatives of all the member states of the United Nations, to be one of its principal organs. The General Assembly is empowered to discuss any questions or matters within the scope of the United Nations' Charter, and to make recommendations to the members of the United Nations or to its Security Council.

The preamble to the United Nations' Charter affirms "faith in fundamental human rights, in the dignity and worth of the human person, [and] in the equal rights of men and women." Article 1 of the Charter identifies respect for human rights as one of the purposes of the organization. Article 55 provides that the United Nations shall promote universal respect for, and observance of, human rights and fundamental freedoms for all without distinction as to race, sex, language, or religion. Article 56 commits member states to take both joint and separate action in cooperation with the United Nations to achieve these goals. The bodies created to fulfil these functions are the United Nations' 'Charter-based' human rights bodies, which include the Human Rights Council (formerly the Commission on Human Rights). Processes and procedures that fall under the remit of the Human Rights Council include the Universal Periodic Review, which periodically measures the performance of every state against relevant standards in the United Nations' Charter and the Universal Declaration of Human Rights; and Special Procedures Mechanisms which address country-specific situations or thematic issues.

Following the adoption of the Universal Declaration, the United Nations' Human Rights Commission was charged with responsibility for drafting a legally binding multilateral treaty for implementing the standard of achievement established by the declaration. Political disagreements about the rights to be recognised resulted in a decision to draft two covenants, rather than a single one, both of which were adopted on 16 December 1966 and came into force in 1976: the International Covenant on Civil and Political Rights and the International Covenant on Economic, Social and Cultural Rights. Since then, a further seven 'core' human rights treaties have been created.* Each one has a body that oversees implementation and compliance in states that have ratified the relevant treaty. The treaty bodies, composed of independent experts, consider state reports, issue general comments, conduct inquiries, and receive complaints.

The Office of the High Commissioner for Human Rights (OHCHR), established in 1994, engages with both the Charter-based human rights bodies and the treaty-based human rights bodies to support human rights standard-setting, monitoring, and implementation. As well as providing technical support and human rights capacity development at the national level, the OHCHR responds to human rights emergencies by deploying monitoring and reporting officers. Since 2014, the OHCHR has pursued six thematic priorities in its work: strengthening human rights mechanisms; enhancing equality and countering discrimination; combating impunity and strengthening accountability and the rule of law; integrating human rights in development and the economic sphere; widening the democratic society space; and early warning and protection of human rights in situations of conflict, violence, and insecurity.

The international system for the protection and promotion of

---

\* A system of more specialised treaties, dealing with specific rights recognised in the Universal Declaration and the two covenants were subsequently concluded: International Convention on the Elimination of All Forms of Racial Discrimination (1965), Convention on the Elimination of All Forms of Discrimination Against Women (1979), Convention Against Torture and Other Cruel, Inhuman or Degrading Treatment or Punishment (1984), Convention on the Rights of the Child (1989), International Convention on the Protection of the Rights of All Migrant Workers and their Families (1990), Convention on the Rights of Persons with Disabilities (2006), International Convention for the Protection of All Persons from Enforced Disappearance (2006). In addition, the Declaration of All Forms of Intolerance and of Discrimination Based on Religion or Belief was proclaimed by the General Assembly in 1981 as a non-binding declaration that further elaborates Article 18 of the International Covenant on Civil and Political Rights.

human rights is sophisticated and multi-tiered. It is possible to point to significant ways in which the global rights regime has advanced human rights in many countries in the period since the signing of the Universal Declaration of Human Rights. Yet it is also the case that in the most urgent and precarious situations, where the basic rights of the most vulnerable are at stake, the system has failed. The twin problems of the politicisation of the global system and the lack of practical enforcement measures have stymied the realisation of rights.

When the focus turns to Australia, it quickly becomes apparent that there is no single point of reference for the protection of human rights in Australian law. The default position of the common law has always been that a person's rights are entitlements to everything that has not been forbidden by parliament or the law. This broad freedom of the individual is not unalienable—it can be limited by ordinary legislation.

There is a small number of rights that are guaranteed by the Australian Constitution, and which cannot be removed by ordinary legislation. These include the right to vote; to trial by jury (in limited circumstances); to non-discrimination based on State of residence; to free trade between the States; to acquisition of property by the Commonwealth on just terms; and freedom from interference with exercise of religion, the imposition of religious observance or religious test for public office or establishment of any religion by the Commonwealth. There is also an implied right of political communication.[1]

There is no constitutional bill of rights in Australia as there is in countries such as the United States. There is also no statutory protection of the kind found in countries such as the United Kingdom, which has the *Human Rights Act 1998*, or New Zealand, which has the *Bill of Rights Act 1990* and the *Human Rights Act 1993*. There is some protection for human rights in state and territory legislation. The Australian Capital Territory's Legislative Assembly enacted the *Human Rights Act 2004* and the Victorian Parliament enacted the *Charter of*

*Human Rights and Responsibilities Act 2006*. In 2019, the Queensland Parliament enacted the *Human Rights Act*.

The Australian Government has signed and ratified numerous international covenants and conventions, but this does not mean that they have been incorporated into domestic law in Australia. This can only be achieved by an act of parliament. Even when international law is not a binding source of law in Australia, it can still exert an influence on the development of the common law and the interpretation of statutes. For example, regard for Australia's international obligations was an important factor in the High Court's decision to abolish the doctrine of terra nullius and recognise native title in Mabo. The *Acts Interpretation Act 1901* anticipates that treaties and international agreements will be used from time to time when interpreting certain statutory provisions. This is particularly the case when the treaty or agreement is explicitly referred to in the statute.

Australia, like many other countries, possesses a National Human Rights Institution (NHRI). Australia's NHRI was established in 1986 as the Human Rights and Equal Opportunity Commission and renamed in 2008 as the Australian Human Rights Commission. The importance of NHRIs stems from their location within the state. NHRIs are (ideally) vectors for the norms of international human rights law, transmitting them from the global sphere of United Nations treaties and treaty bodies to the domestic arena where they can be promoted through education, protected in legislation, and enforced by the executive. Because of their accessibility, independent and well-resourced institutions, which possess a broad mandate and wide-ranging powers, have the potential to significantly increase the level of human rights protection afforded to citizens.[2] Australia's NHRI has published significant studies on Indigenous deaths in custody; the removal of Indigenous children from their families since the 1930s; sexual harassment and discrimination in the workplace; and treatment of the disabled and mentally ill in institutions.

The state and territory legislatures have also enacted statutes that seek to prevent discrimination and otherwise to promote human rights within their jurisdictions. In each case, statutory bodies have been established for this purpose.

The Commonwealth Parliament's *Human Rights (Parliamentary Scrutiny) Act 2011* provides for a parliamentary Joint Committee on Human Rights, which is required to examine all proposed laws for compatibility with the aforementioned international covenants and conventions to which Australia is a party. The committee is required to advise the Parliament on whether a proposed law complies with Australia's international obligations.

On 10 December 2008, the Australian Government announced that it would conduct a National Human Rights Consultation. The terms of reference stated three broad questions:

- Which human rights (including corresponding responsibilities) should be protected and promoted?
- Are these human rights currently sufficiently protected and promoted?
- How could Australia better protect and promote human rights?

A committee, chaired by Father Frank Brennan, was established to conduct the consultation and prepare a report. The report acknowledged that there is significant controversy surrounding the implementation of human rights protection in Australia. One area of such controversy related to 'hot button' topics such as same-sex marriage, euthanasia, and abortion; another area of controversy related to the appropriateness of introducing a Human Rights Act in Australia. Ultimately, the Committee recommended that Australia *should* adopt a federal Human Rights Act. This recommendation, however, was not accepted. Arguments against the introduction of a Human Rights Act included concerns that an Act would elevate and politicise the role of the judiciary and increase contentious rights-based litigation. The Consultation exposed the complex and contested place of human rights in Australian social and political life.

In his prologue to this volume, Michael Casey sets out his thesis that current approaches to human rights are at risk of devaluing the currency of human rights in the longer term. He does not reach a conclusion, but he poses a question, the answer to which might suggest further reasons for being concerned that human rights are at risk of becoming nonsense on stilts. Even if there were no theoretical problem with the foundations for human rights, treatment of human rights in the legal and political processes, and popular perceptions of human rights, might mean that human rights are still at risk of becoming nonsense on stilts for these reasons. So there is a need to rescue human rights in Australia. This volume is an attempt at thinking about how to rescue human rights in Australia. It does so both by accepting some of the concerns—in the essay by Damien Freeman—and by refuting them—in the essay by Catherine Renshaw. Finally, Nicholas Aroney, Terri Butler, Jennifer Cook, Emma Dawson, Bryan Turner, and Tim Wilson respond to the essays by Freeman and Renshaw.

Damien Freeman purports to diagnose the reason why human rights has become nonsense on stilts and to prescribe a cure that can rescue it. He distinguishes between 'rights' and 'interests', and argues that rights are 'trumps' that are intended to end conversations. He argues that politics should be concerned with having conversations about human interests, but there is no place for rights in such conversations, as they end conversations, rather than encouraging conversations about important human interests. So he argues that the Australian Human Rights Commission needs to be reformed, and the Australian Parliament's Joint Committee on Human Rights needs to be abolished in order to promote greater political discussion about human interests.

Catherine Renshaw agrees that there is a malady in need of diagnosis, but she fundamentally rejects Freeman's diagnosis, and hence also his prescription for a cure. She argues that what is needed is greater consensus about human rights, and she sees deliberative democracy as the best way of achieving this. Thus, she argues that constraints on deliberative democracy are the gravest threat to human rights. Rescuing them requires increased deliberative democracy, and she regards institutions such as the Australian Human Rights Commission as critical to fostering participatory democracy and the consensus that can flow from it.

Two current members of the House of Representatives in the Parliament of the Commonwealth of Australia then respond to the approaches of Freeman and Renshaw. Terri Butler discusses the role that human rights plays in the deliberations of parliament, and in doing so defends the role of the Joint Committee on Human Rights. Tim Wilson draws not only on his experience in parliament, but also on his time as Human Rights Commissioner, to argue that what is needed in parliament and beyond is an ongoing conversation about human rights that is focussed on those that promote Sir Isaiah Berlin's concept of 'negative liberty', rather than those associated with 'positive liberty'.

Emma Dawson and Nicholas Aroney contribute two alternative perspectives from outside the political arena about the politics of rescuing human rights. Aroney believes that Freeman is on the right track, although he does not go far enough in his diagnosis, observing that the ills of human rights talk also fail in a significant way to take seriously the place of institutions, as well as individuals, when thinking about human flourishing. Dawson, on the other hand, utterly rejects Freeman's cure, and seeks to demonstrate that he has not provided a meaningful argument for reforming the Human Rights Commission and abolishing the Joint Committee on Human Rights.

Finally, we come to the last pair of essays by Jennifer Cook and Bryan Turner. Cook agrees with Renshaw that there is a need for greater participatory democracy. She argues that international human rights law can provide the solution, but that domestic politics prevents this in Australia, because the legislature restrains a judiciary that is increasingly sympathetic to international human rights jurisprudence from engaging seriously with this body of law when making determinations about Australian law. Turner identifies the problem not so much in the attitude of Australian lawmakers to international human rights law, so much as in their attitude to the differing treatment of Australian citizens, 'quasi-citizens', 'sub-citizens', and 'non-citizens', which leads him to think the real issue has more to do with a difference between human rights and citizenship rights.

In 2009, after reviewing 35,000 written submissions and conducting four months of consultations across the breadth of Australia, the National Human Rights Consultation Committee reported to the Australian Parliament its clearest finding:

> Australians know little about their human rights—what they are, where they come from and how they are protected. They need and want education. They need and want to create a better culture of human rights in those organisations that deliver public services to the community.[3]

This collection of essays shows, that in the decade since that statement was made, our understanding about what human rights are has become murkier and the path to rescuing human rights has become even less clear. In the face of philosophical and religious pluralism, there are very few people who still cleave to the traditional natural law understanding of human rights. There are very many people who are willing to recognise the difficulties inherent in trying to create a coherent body of principles from disparate understandings about the nature of rights. And there are none, it seems, who are willing to deny that human rights are necessary and that failure to adequately protect them is a terrible injustice.

These essays contain much learning, but much learning is often accompanied by much nonsense. At that venerable seat of learning, All Souls College, Oxford, nonsense erupts once every hundred years, when the Lord Mallard leads a nocturnal procession around the college, proudly singing the Mallard Song in a ceremony known as Hunting the Mallard. On 15 January 2001, the *Telegraph* reported:

> Some of Oxford's most learned fellows were marching around their college behind a wooden duck held aloft on a pole, after excessive eating and drinking, late last night. The bizarre ritual of 'hunting the mallard' occurs once every hundred years at All Souls College in commemoration of the chase after a huge wild duck which flew from a drain during fifteenth-century building works. Archbishop Henry Chichele, who established All Souls in 1438, is said to have had a premonition about the duck in a dream.

The last time the ritual had been performed was in 1901, when Cosmo Gordon Lang served as Lord Mallard. It was a precursor to the pivotal role that he would have in an even grander ritual thirty-six years later, when, as Archbishop of Canterbury, he crowned King George VI. Lang records in his memoirs:

> I was carried in a chair by four stalwart Fellows—Wilbrahim [First Church Estates Commissioner], Gwyer [later Chief Justice of India], Steel-Maitland [later Minister of Labour] and Fossie Cunliffe—for nearly two hours after midnight round the quadrangles and roofs of the College, with a dead mallard borne in front on a long pole (which I still possess) singing the Mallard Song all the time, preceded by the seniors and followed by the juniors, all of them carrying staves and torches, a scene unimaginable in any place in the world except Oxford, or there in any society except All Souls.

Lang's biographer, J. G. Lockhart, observed, "Such elaborate junketing may sound a little odd to anyone unconnected with All Souls . . . But presumably, if Homer may be excused an occasional nod, a Fellow of All Souls may be allowed, once in a hundred years, to play the fool."

Australian Catholic University still yearns for its place in the sun. All Souls College it may not be either in learning or nonsense. It has no mallard. Instead its art collection has to make do with the duck decanter made of amber glass and silver plate, and attributed to Karel Palda, a Czech craftsman, circa 1900, which graces the cover of this volume. We mortals can but wonder what nonsense occurs in some elysian plain, two hours after midnight, when the Vice-Chancellor, carried in a chair by select Fellows of Senate and preceded by Their Graces the Archbishops of Sydney and Melbourne with croziers in hand, processes with the fully charged duck decanter borne in front by the Professors of Catholic Philosophy and Canon Law. It is a scene imaginable only at ACU.

The Universal Declaration of Human Rights is no Mallard Song, and human rights are no frolic. What is at stake is too serious to allow us to console ourselves that even Homer nods. It is true that not even the most vigilant and expert are immune to error. If they have allowed human rights in Australia to become derided as nonsense on stilts, however, then it behoves us to ask how human rights can be rescued.

# Two approaches to rescuing human rights in Australia

# In the long grass

Damien Freeman

Philip Larkin's poetry gives expression to the tone of post-war Britain in all its weary and mundane smallness. In the celebrated poem, "An Arundel Tomb", he reminds us of our "almost-instinct" about the significance of love. In "This Be The Verse", he warns of the enduring misery that is the legacy of family life. "High Windows" offers insights into the transcendent. Yet, it is not in his meditations on love, family, or the transcendent that the foundation of our life in common is disclosed. Rather, this is found in the long grass he was mowing when a wild hedgehog got jammed between the blades of his lawnmower.

"We should be careful of each other," Larkin ends his poem, "The Mower", admonishing us, "we should be kind while there is still time."[1] In this twelve-line poem, he recounts the time he was mowing the lawn and found a hedgehog that had been grazing in the long grass "jammed up against the blades, Killed." The poem is a meditation on the poet's grief process. He recalls having seen the hedgehog and having fed it, and he laments the way that he has so violently—albeit unintentionally—"mauled" this unobtrusive creature. He buries the hedgehog, but that does not help. The following day he is grieving over the loss that he has caused, and this grief prompts him to conclude the poem by imploring us to be kinder to one another.

Larkin's sentimental attachment to a wild animal that he had encountered only briefly leads him to a realisation about his sentimental attachment to other people; not just the people with whom he is intimately connected, but all of us. We should be as kind to others as we would have them be kind to the hedgehog in the long grass. Perhaps, this is a peculiar inversion of the Golden Rule suited to our times.

The power of Larkin's feeling for the mauled hedgehog is instructive. It gestures us towards a more profound feeling for our fellow creatures; a feeling that the late twentieth-century American philosopher, Richard Rorty, suggests can be harnessed to provide an anchor for human rights.

In his contribution to the Oxford Amnesty Lectures for 1993, *On Human Rights*,[2] Rorty is captivated by a report written by David Rieff in 1992 on the situation in Bosnia:

> To the Serbs, the Muslims are no longer human. . . . Muslim prisoners, lying on the ground in rows, awaiting interrogation, were driven over by a Serb guard in a small delivery van. . . . A Muslim man in Bosansi Petrovac . . . [was] forced to bite off the penis of a fellow-Muslim... If you say that a man is not human, but the man looks like you and the only way to identify this devil is to make him drop his trousers—Muslim men are circumcised and Serb men are not—it is probably only a short step, psychologically, to cutting off his prick. . . . There has never been a campaign of ethnic cleansing from which sexual sadism has gone missing.[3]

Rorty is taken by the thought that the Serbs would never do such things to fellow human beings, but only to *Muslims*. The point is that they can distinguish between true humans and pseudohumans, and because Muslims are regarded as pseudohumans, these are not crimes against humanity. One response is to demonstrate the obvious to the Serbs: that Muslims are in fact humans, and to do so by pointing out their humanity—the essential characteristic that Muslims share with all other humans but which is lacking in hedgehogs and other animals. Rorty traces this approach back to Kant, and ultimately to Plato, who claimed that the essence of humanity is rationality. Rorty believes that such an approach is doomed, however, because it is not possible to provide a compelling answer to the question, What is the essence of being human? It is for this reason that he believes it is impossible to provide a foundation for human rights.

Rorty does believe that we should be kind to one another, and not treat our fellow humans as if they were animals rather than humans. He does not think, however, that there is any fact, such as that "we are the disobedient children of a loving God, or that human beings differ from other kinds of animals by having dignity rather than mere value", that justifies our doing so.[4] Rather, he thinks it is experiences such as Larkin's encounter with the hedgehog in the long grass that motivate us to commit ourselves to treating each other as humans rather than pseudohumans:

> We pragmatists argue from the fact that the emergence of the human rights culture seems to owe nothing to increased moral knowledge, and everything to hearing sad and sentimental stories, to the conclusion that there is probably no knowledge of the sort Plato envisaged. We go on to argue: Since no useful work seems to be done by insisting on a purportedly ahistorical human nature, there probably is no such nature, or at least nothing in that nature that is relevant to our moral choices.[5]

When asked, "What makes us different from the other animals?" Rorty claims we should not provide an answer to the question. Rather, we should simply assert: "We can feel *for each other* to a much greater extent than they can."[6] Thus, what matters is that Larkin comes to feel something for his fellow humans that the hedgehog could never feel. Rorty thinks this is at the core of our commitment to human rights: we come to feel a certain way about one another, and that feeling anchors us to a commitment to a human rights culture. If this is so, what matters, he suggests, is concentrating "our energies on manipulating sentiments, on sentimental education. That sort of education sufficiently acquaints people of different kinds with one another so that they are less tempted to think of those different from themselves as only quasi-human." In this way, he proposes that we can "expand the reference of the terms 'our kind of people' and 'people like us.'"[7] Thus, Rorty speculates that an Enlightenment utopia will come about through a liberal education that manipulates students' "sentiments in such a way that they imagine themselves in the shoes of the despised and oppressed" so as to produce "generations of nice, tolerant, well-off, secure, other-respecting students of this sort in all parts of the world".[8]

Even giving Rorty his claim that it is sentiment rather than rationality that provides an anchor for our appreciating the humanity of one another, how far does this get us in terms of our commitment to human rights? Can Serbs make the move from feeling that Muslims are human, and should be treated as such, to the belief that Muslims have human rights? Should Serbs be encouraged to make this move? Or is there a better move for them to make?

It is one thing to say that human rights are rights that pertain to human beings, just as animal rights are rights that pertain to animals. It is quite another to say that human rights are rights that people have *in virtue of* being human, just as animal rights are rights that hedgehogs have in virtue of their animality.[9] Rorty thinks he can show us that sentiment can get us to the first claim even though it cannot get us as far as the second claim. Raymond Geuss, a contemporary political theorist and scholar of European philosophy, thinks that it is a mistake, however, even to try and make the first claim. This is because, whereas Rorty thinks the problems of human rights are centred on the *human*, Geuss thinks they are centred on the *rights*.

It is hardly controversial that human beings have an interest in many things, including their prosperity, security, and liberty. A sentimental education may incline us towards a better appreciation of both the range of interests that we share, and the range of people with whom we share such interests. The more we understand about our shared interests, the kinder we might feel towards our fellow humans.

The more kindly we are disposed, the more we might wish to affirm the interests of fellow humans. That may have implications for our culture. But it does not get us to the point at which we can assert that our fellow human beings have human *rights* that are in need of protection. Rather, it gets us to the point at which we can appreciate that we should be concerned about the *interests* of our fellow human beings.

Geuss argues that it would be a fundamental mistake to make the move from being concerned about human interests to asserting that these interests constitute human rights. He objects to this move because of his understanding of what rights are: "Rights are not processes. Rights are trumps, they stop the process. Now in some contexts that might be the best you can get. However politics is about processes, and our aspiration should be to make those processes as participatory as possible."[10] He believes that what matters is "collective forms of agency, collective powers, and collective forms of suffering" and that discussion of rights takes "attention away from these other important things," when we should be discussing "who the agencies will be, and how co-operation will be structured. It's to take our attention away from finding forms of living together which won't require giving trumps to people."[11]

If, as Geuss believes, rights are trumps, then rights discourse confuses law and politics, because trumps stop discussion: "Another way to say that is that they're unpolitical. They're an attempt to shift from politics into legalism, to give a legal model for politics."[12] Rights "are supposed to hold for everyone in all situations," but this means that by their very nature they cannot "take account of the peculiarities of individual situations" whereas "in some sense all political situations are individual." Rights also fail politically because they put "different things at the same level: a right to life, a right to education, a right to entertainment. These are not necessarily things on the same level in human life or in politics." What matters in politics, however, is "to think about the differential importance of things, to say there's nothing but rights . . . levels out significant qualitative differences."[13]

Human rights might be asserted in international relations, or within the domestic law of a given nation state, and Geuss is aware that these might create their own problems. He has a particular objection to the introduction of the idea of human rights within the domain of domestic politics, however, because he thinks it is ill-suited to the purpose of politics: "To set priorities, to have conflicts, to override some claims in particular cases, that's what politics is about." Rights-discourse seeks to stop such debate, "So it's an inherently apolitical way of thinking about politics. It's a particularly clumsy, crude and rigid attempt to turn politics into a kind of administration or legal discussion."[14] Geuss understands that "it is tempting to think about human life in that way, and why in some context it might even be important" but he insists that "it's not the right way *finally* to think about politics."[15]

The common law is based upon the idea that people can have rights. This is the basis of property ownership and of our form of society. Rights have characteristics fitted to the legal domain in which they belong: "Rights by their very nature must be crude. They can't be subtle or highly differentiated because they're legal functions . . . but politics should be about making people more differentiated." Geuss maintains that politics "shouldn't be about just making block-like demands, such as: 'protect my property', it should be about thinking about what in this city is the right rate of investment in education, in health; how we should structure new forms of urban development; where we should build schools and hospitals" because "You can't reduce that to mere demands for rights." He concedes that legal structures, in contrast, need to be "coarse-grained . . . processes that are verifiably repeatable and that are subject to public scrutiny." It is a recurring theme for Geuss that political processes should be more differentiated than legal processes, and that "politics should be about something more than merely claiming rights." Politics, he says, "should aim at activating people."[16]

Rorty might be right that our sentiments lead us to appreciate the range of interests that we share with our fellow humans, but should we understand these interests as rights? Geuss is adamant that this would be a mistake because rights discourse is "a trap, to be more exact, it is a trap because it tries to construe political situations as apolitical."[17] When it comes to human interests, it is important that we should have conversations about these interests. We need to discuss which interests should be affirmed and how people's interests can flourish: education might be demanded because it is "an important way of satisfying our interests. Or we say we have a need for it. That is a more perspicuous way of saying something important than by speaking of 'rights'. By calling it a right you don't add anything to calling it a satisfaction of a basic need or an important demand or a vital human interest."

> If, on the other hand, you talk about education as being an important thing for people, as being a human need, this way of speaking moves you on constructively to an interesting political discussion. If I say it is an important need that I have an education, then you ask me, "why is it a need?", then I will talk about my needs, and this will naturally lead to discussion of other aspects of my life. That's a political way of formulating the demand. If I say, "it's a right" I'm immediately saying it's a trump, that is something I don't discuss, it's something that's limited, it's something that's rigid and determinate, it's something to stop the political discussion, it's inviolable, and so on.[18]

Geuss admits that sometimes "it might be good to be irrational" or adopt "non-negotiable ways", but to do so betrayals something central to the project of politics. He wants to encourage us to have conversations about human interests and how we can promote them. Thus, Geuss advocates a departure from rights discourse in politics and calls for us to replace it with 'good' politics: "Think about what good politics is. . . . [It addresses] human agency, human interests, human powers, human needs . . . [This provides] a much more fruitful and forward-looking way of approaching politics, than through obsession with rights."[19]

Geuss offers a Marxist critique of human rights, rather than a libertarian critique, but he is well aware of the overlap between the two. Political agency in a healthy state is not restricted to the election of formal representatives, but should include different kinds of associations and ways of doing politics:

> To give priority to claiming rights gives us the completely wrong attitude toward ourselves, other political agencies and the state because it basically prioritises us as passive clients of the nanny-state. This idea of a 'nanny-state' is a conservative[†] invention, but what is wrong with it is the tacit (and utterly implausible form of) atomistic individualism that stands behind it and the irrational suspicion of any form of collective organisation. It does, however, contain the germ of a correct perception about the deleterious effects of the potential passivity of modern populations. If all we do is vote, and then shout for mama whenever someone treads on our toes, saying, "This is my land; I claim this right, I claim that right, I claim the other right", that is a really very narrow way of thinking about what politics can do and be. And if you take that as your central way of thinking about politics you're going to have a tremendously distorted and impoverished form of politics.[20]

Should our life in common be organised around conversations about human interests, as Geuss suggests, or around stopping conversations about human interests as human rights discourse requires? Two domains of public life take different approaches to answering this question.

At the core of the legal system is the idea that there are interests

---

† What Geuss describes as a conservative critique, I would prefer to describe as a libertarian critique. In *Abbott's Right*, I discuss the libertarian commitment to a form of atomistic individualism that Geuss rightly claims to be implausible. As I am at pains to explain in that book, genuine conservatives do not share this ideological commitment of libertarians. Although conservatives in the tradition of Burke will value liberty, the basis for their commitment is different from that of libertarians. When I discuss Julian Leeser below, I regard him as a Burkean conservative rather than a libertarian.

about which we should not have conversations, and these are recognised as legal rights. If a litigant goes to court and asserts a right, and the court is satisfied of the validity of that right, then the court will end any further discussion about it. Law courts are not places to discuss human interests. They are places to end discussions about human interests. That courts should declare rights rather than have conversations about human interests is critical for the rule of law. The rule of law depends upon legal certainty; that similar cases will be judged similarly, and that outcomes can be predicted. Such certainty is achievable when a court declares pre-existing rights, in a way that it is not possible in conversations about human interests, which will always have greater volatility.

That political conversations about human interests are volatile need not be a weakness within a political system that does not depend for its authority upon certainty of political outcomes. The ministry deals with politics, and its business is concerned with having conversations about human interests. These conversations might be volatile, but this does not undermine its authority, which lies in its accountability to the parliament, and which in turn has a democratic mandate. So the executive can afford to be a conversation starter, rather than a conversation stopper, when it comes to human interests. The judiciary, in contrast, must be a conversation stopper rather than a conversation starter.

The parliament is situated at the intersection of law and politics. It makes the laws that are enforced by the judiciary and holds the executive to account for political decisions. So the legislature has a role both in starting conversations about human interests (through its political dimension) and in stopping conversations about human interests (through its legal dimension). The legislature should be regulating the right mixture of law and conversation.

There is any number of ways in which a constitution might provide for the domains in which law and politics are conducted. We are familiar with constitutions that spread these across the legislature, the executive, and the judiciary. Montesquieu's classic conception of these organs of government is that each exercises a distinctive form of power, and that the separation of powers is a doctrine according to which assigning each form of power to a separate organ provides for a system in which each serves as a check on the other. This traditional approach, which A. V. Dicey maintains goes hand-in-hand with the rule of law, comes under a powerful attack in the work of Sir Ivor Jennings, who argues that what distinguishes the executive from the judiciary is not that it exercises a different form of power, but that it operates according to different processes.

Whereas Dicey and Jennings disagree about the nature of the distinction between the executive and the judiciary, Walter Bagehot sees a quite different distinction as being fundamental in *The English Constitution*.[21] He emphasises the distinction between the efficient parts of the English constitution (which include both the executive and the judiciary) and the dignified parts. What this suggests is that, depending upon the purpose of one's inquiry, different distinctions might seem more or less important. For some purposes, what matters is whether the courts and the ministry exercise judicial or executive power; for other purposes, what matters is whether they are efficient or dignified parts of the constitution. For present purposes, a third distinction seems to be most fundamental, namely whether they operate in the domain of law or the domain of politics.

If one accepts this analysis of the assertion of rights in the domain of law and conversation about human interests in the domain of politics, concerns about human rights in Australia can then be approached through a discussion of the institutions through which human rights are currently protected in Australia, and whether they operate appropriately in the domain of politics and the domain of law. The discussion then moves from one of political theory to political science. How does the domain of politics currently deal with human interests in Australia? Are we satisfied with the way political institutions function, or are they in need of reform? The following case study suggests that at least one politician believes that there is a problem with the approach that two institutions take to human rights. When we unpack his arguments, what becomes apparent is that the foregoing discussion of political theory provides a basis for understanding this politician's calls for reform of Australia's human rights institutions.

In his 2018 B'nai B'rith Lecture, the federal Member for Berowra, Julian Leeser, takes aim at the way human rights are currently protected in Australia.[22] Whereas Geuss is a Marxist, and is opposed to property rights which, like religion, Marxists claim are used by capitalists as a tool of suppression, Leeser is committed to property rights, commercial society, and religion. So he is not opposed in principle to the recognition of any human interests as human rights. What he opposes is the way in which some human interests are currently translated into human rights in Australia. Leeser takes aim at two domestic human rights institutions: the Australian Human Rights Commission and the Australian Parliament's Joint Committee on Human Rights. He argues that the first needs to be reformed and the second abolished.

Leeser argues that the Human Rights Commission has lost public support due to political activists who have "brought proceedings which had no real prospects of success, and a Human Rights Commission which failed to exercise its powers". This has "weakened public confidence in the Racial Discrimination Act and has removed bipartisan support from these provisions." The Commission, he argues, was "designed to be one of our most compelling moral voices" but finds itself "under sustained attack because it is, and has pretty much always been, adventurous and partisan. . . . No institution can survive without broad community support and the Human Rights Commission is skating on thin ice. Too much of its output fails to pass the pub test."

That a commitment to a common standard of achievement can quickly become a trump card is at the core of Leeser's critique. The point is not that the commission should apply the pub test to resolve difficult problems, but that it should have regard to the pub test. It should be seeking solutions that are in keeping with the pub test and, at the same time, in keeping with the international instruments that the commission is charged with responsibility for upholding. This need not be an either/or situation. The commission has an obligation to facilitate conciliation between a complainant and a respondent when a complaint is lodged with the commission. This needs to be a four-way process. It needs to have regard to the interests of the complainant and the interests of the respondent. In doing so, it needs to have regard to the common standard of achievement for all peoples and all nations that it is the Universal Declaration of Human Rights, which the commission is charged with upholding in Australia. It also needs to have regard to the circumstances of Australian society—what might be called the pub test. No one of these four considerations should be regarded as a trump.

Compelling moral voices should seek to have meaningful discussions about human interests, and to bring about a conciliation when one person's human interests seem to be compromised by the actions of another. This process should have regard for the internationally sanctioned common standard of achievement to which Australia has committed itself. But it should also have regard for the conditions of Australian society in which this common standard needs to be applied, which is where the pub test comes in.

The commission will always be a political player—how can it not be, when it is charged with having conversations about human interests, and such conversations are an inherently political activity. To address Leeser's criticism that, as a political player, the commission has lost broad community support, the commission needs to accept that it does not hold trumps in its hand. For as long as the commission conceives of itself as safeguarding *rights*, it will continue to lose broad community support. That is the whole point of rights: they are trumps that end conversations. So, as long as the commission understands itself as the protector of rights, it will remain committed to stopping conversations and so undermining confidence in the political process.

If the commission understands the international instruments that it upholds as articulating a set of vital human interests, then it is open to the commission to encourage parties towards a conciliation that respects those interests, and which at the same time is cognizant of other considerations relevant to Australian society in reaching a settlement about how these interests can be accommodated in particular circumstances. This would require a kind of restraint on the part of those charged with responsibility for the Australian Human Rights Commission Act and associated legislation, but it would instill broader community support for these institutions. In short, the commission needs to commit itself to starting conversations about human interests rather than insisting that certain conversations about human interests be stopped. In the rare circumstances in which a human interest is recognised legally as a right, it is appropriate for the courts to stop conversations. Beyond those limited cases, however, what is required of the commission is a conversation about options for reconciling competing interests.

Leeser offers a stronger critique of the Human Rights (Parliamentary Scrutiny) Act, which he believes is incapable of being reformed and so must be repealed. He points out that every bill that is introduced into the parliament needs to be scrutinized for compatibility with seven international treaties which, he says, "have no protections for freedom of contract or property rights—the rights on which our entire Australian legal system is based." However, "these treaties do protect the right to 'enjoy the benefits of scientific progress and its applications', the right to holiday pay, paid maternity leave; free education; the right to social security; and the right to an 'adequate standard of living'." He asks rhetorically, "These things might be nice to have but really would most Australians consider them to be human rights? And more so than the right to property and freedom of contract?"

Not only does he object to the committee's mandate, Leeser also objects to the committee's procedures, explaining, "I do not believe it is truly a committee of the parliament. I believe it is a bureaucracy that has appropriated the name of the parliament. The committee is about bureaucrats judging parliament, rather than the parliament judging human rights." He says that should committee members disagree with the scrutiny report prepared by the bureaucrats, they are told, "this is not about the rights or wrongs of the legislation, this is merely a technical assessment of the human rights implications of the law." Unlike other parliamentary committees, he claims that this committee does not canvas, test, or weigh up alternative views and evidence, and he concludes that "by removing discretion the committee represents an attack on the fundamental liberties for which the parliament is supposed to stand."

The Human Rights (Parliamentary Scrutiny) Act is not mistaken when it recognises that the seven international instruments identify human interests to which proposed legislation should have regard. The mistake is to conceive of them as the kind of human interests about which we must stop all conversation. Most Australians would agree that these are human interests, some of which might seem more pressing to some Australians than to other Australians. Most Australians would consider these to be interests about which we can have a conversation. Genocide is also a violation of human interests. There are no ifs or buts about genocide: we cannot have a conversation about when it is justified and when it is not. Many—if not all—Australians have an interest in scientific progress, holiday pay, maternity leave, free education, social security, and an adequate standard of living. But these are all human interests about which we can have a conversation, and indeed about which we should have conversations. There are different ways of addressing these different human interests, and it is right that we have conversations about the best way of promoting such interests.

That is to say, however, that we should be starting conversations about these things, rather than stopping conversations about them. It is a feature of the way Leeser reports that the committee operates that it serves to stop conversations about these human interests by declaring them rights. This is the problem. We cannot morally have a conversation about when to permit genocide, but we should have a conversation about promoting people's interests in science, holiday pay and maternity leave, education, social security, and standards of living. To designate these as rights, however, is to stop any conversation about them.

The problem worsens when the committee serves to stifle conversation about these human interests in the very forum in which the conversation should be had. It is the role of the legislature to conduct political conversations about human interests; to decide how these interests should be promoted; and to decide when further conversation about a particular human interest is unacceptable, by declaring it to be a right which can be enforced by the courts which terminates any further discussion about that interest. There is no place in our parliamentary system for a bureaucracy that frustrates this in the very forum that is supposed to work out how to advance human interests within Australian society; the forum that needs to decide when it is necessary to authorise the courts to stop further discussion about certain interests that are designated as rights.

Leeser raises the proposed legislation regarding cashless welfare card trials for social security recipients as an example of the problem, explaining that the committee's report claimed that the trials "limited the right of social security, the right of privacy and family and the right of equality and non-discrimination". What he finds particularly offensive about this approach is its failure to consider the rights of women and children who suffer domestic abuse at the hands of men who misuse the payments to support gambling and alcohol addictions. He says, "This committee always puts the rights of the offender over the rights of the community.... I don't want to be part of a committee that elevates the rights of deadbeat dads and child sex offenders and fails to consider the safety of the community."

Even deadbeat dads and sex offenders have some legitimate interests worthy of advancement notwithstanding their misconduct. The problem is that once these interests are characterized as rights, they must trump any other interests, such as the safety of the community, and so a committee that recognises such interests as *rights* has no choice but to insist that conversation about limiting the deadbeat dads and sex offenders' interests must end.

"By seeing human rights in almost every piece of legislation," Leeser says, "the committee has become the boy who cried wolf." The committee is entirely right, however, in seeing human interests in every piece of legislation. What would be the point of enacting legislation if it did not touch on some human interest? The mistake lies in the failure to see that every human interest is not a human right. If the interest at stake is genuinely a right, then the committee should act to shut down conversation about that interest. But if it is a human interest about which the parliament should be having a conversation, rather than one about which it should end further conversation, then it is a mistake to characterize the interest as a right, and, by doing so, the committee does cry wolf. The mere fact that the English translation of the Universal Declaration uses the expression *human rights* when reciting the list that constitutes the standard for achievement does not change the fact that the members of the Australian parliament must have conversations about promoting these interests in Australia. It does not legitimize anyone telling the members of the Australian parliament that they must stop further conversation about these human interests.

Leeser contrasts his experience on the Joint Committee on Human Rights with his experience on the Joint Committee for Intelligence and Security. Both committees were required to consider government proposals for legislation on foreign interference. The Human Rights Committee apparently published a report containing "regurgitated third-party talking points warning the parliament of the human rights dangers of seeking to protect our country from nefarious outside state-sponsored influence", and then approved the report within "a matter of minutes". In contrast, the Intelligence and Security Committee "took seven months, held six public hearings and two private hearings, reviewed 92 submissions, had months of internal debate among committee members". All of this, Leeser explains, aimed at balancing "liberty and security with the fine details of the law", resulting in fifty recommendations to improve the bill.

The crux of the contrast can be located in the different treatment of the rights and interests. The Intelligence and Security Committee treats liberty and security as human interests, both of which are important, and about which it is appropriate to have a conversation. So it is possible to weigh up the competing interests and make recommendations about how the proposed legislation might best promote them. The Human Rights Committee takes a different conceptual approach, and identifies human rights rather than human interests. Once it has done this, it has shut down the possibility of further discussion. For the one committee, liberty is a human interest about which it is important to have a conversation; for the other, it is a right which must be protected by ending further conversation.

This experience forms the basis for Leeser's proposal to abolish the Human Rights Committee. Parliamentarians, he explains, "have not just a responsibility to their communities, but to the nation and to history. You cannot and must not outsource this deep responsibility." Abolishing the committee would constitute a resumption of responsibility: "the parliament would not be turning its back on human rights but it would be turning its back on the bureaucratization of human rights." Another way of formulating this would be to say that the parliament would not be turning its back on human interests, but it would be committing itself to having conversations about human interests, rather than stopping itself from having such conversations. The bureaucratization of human rights necessarily stops conversations in the parliament about human interests. By authorizing a bureaucracy to declare that a right would be violated by proposed legislation, the parliament allows the bureaucracy to stop further discussion about the proposed legislation's treatment of a particular human interest that the bureaucracy has declared to be a right. This should come as no surprise. The whole point of declaring an interest to be a right is to stop conversation. The thrust of Leeser's approach is to remind us that the parliament has an obligation to the nation and to history to have conversations about vital human interests, and it cannot turn its back on this by authorizing a bureaucracy to stop further conversation by proclaiming a human interest to be a human right.

Leeser concludes that the committee cannot be reformed and so it needs to be abolished. It cannot be reformed "because it elevates treaties . . . which have received little public debate such that *every* law is assessed against them. Australians have never agreed that the right to holiday pay or to the benefit of scientific progress are such important rights that they need to be elevated and given effectively such quasi-constitutional status."

The problem is not, however, that every law is assessed against treaty obligations. The problem is that the bureaucracy uses the treaties in a way that aims at stopping conversation about human interests through the device of declaring those interests to be rights. Australians may disagree about the relative importance of holiday pay and the benefit of scientific progress. What matters, however, is that they never agreed that further conversation about how best to promote their interest in holiday pay or their interest in the benefits of scientific progress should be stopped. The committee accords quasi-constitutional status to these human interests when it attempts to stop conversations in the parliament by declaring the human interests affected by proposed legislation to be human rights. When Australia signed up to these international agreements, no one would have expected that doing so would result in a bureaucracy trying to stop the parliament from having conversations about how to promote the human interests identified in the international agreements. So it is reasonable to call for the abolition of the Human Rights Committee, whilst still being committed to having conversations about how the aspirations of these international agreements can be realized in Australia's domestic law.

Leeser also contends that "equating real human rights abuses like massacres in Syria with asking a drunken sailor in Jervis Bay to take a random breath test, and calling the latter a breach of human rights cheapens the real abuses." It is a feature of rights discourse that it elevates all human interests that are accorded the status of rights to the same level, and so it becomes difficult to rank the abuse of one interest against the abuse of another. The deeper problem, however, is that the committee's approach obscures the fact that you have to stop a conversation about the appropriateness of massacres in Syria, whereas you can have a conversation about the appropriateness of asking a drunken sailor to take a random breath test. There are more and less appropriate ways of administering random breath tests in Jervis Bay. There are no more appropriate ways of conducting massacres in Syria. So it is right for the members of the parliament to have a conversation about the most appropriate way of administering the breath test and it is right for them to pass laws that stop further conversation about the circumstances in which massacres in Syria are appropriate. This is the reason why the Syrian example can be said to involve the violation of a genuine right, whereas the Jervis Bay example cannot. A less appropriate way of administering the breath test would needlessly undermine the sailor's vital human interests. So it is appropriate for parliamentarians to have a careful conversation about the interests protected by the breath test and the sailor's human interests that might be unnecessarily compromised by it. But the fact that it is appropriate to have such a conversation reveals that the sailor's interests do not constitute rights. In contrast, the Syrian victims' interests are such that the parliament cannot have a conversation about the appropriateness of their violation, and so their interests do constitute rights. Thus, the parliament should authorize the courts to recognise such interests as rights and to stop further conversation about them.

Finally, Leeser concludes that "other committees are actually doing detailed work considering real human issues through orthodox committee processes weighing up evidence and submissions with committee members exercising discretion and making recommendations to improve legislation such that this committee's very existence makes a mockery of the parliament's consideration of human rights." What he calls the orthodox committee processes for considering real human issues are nothing other than conversations about important human interests. The mockery that lies at the heart of the Human Rights Committee is that, by allowing a bureaucracy to declare human interests to be human rights, the committee system is thwarted because it thereby stops conversations about real human issues in the parliament, rather than encouraging conversations about them.

Michael Casey has drawn attention to a concern that we risk compromising the force of the moral claims made in the name of human rights when we start to recognise contingent requirements for human flourishing as absolute requirements for human flourishing, and, in doing so, dub them 'human rights'. This can create a tension between some more recently recognised human rights and other long-established human rights, in which some human rights have to be disallowed or rejected.

Casey's concern becomes clearer when human rights discourse is analysed in terms of starting and stopping conversations about human interests. By elevating contingent human interests to the status of absolute requirements of human existence, the human interest is translated into a human right, and hence a trump that stops further conversation. We should have conversations about how we can promote people's human interests that contribute to their flourishing. People will lose confidence in law and politics when their institutions stop conversations about human interests that people believe they should be having. If an institution inappropriately characterises a human interest that is properly a contingent requirement as an absolute requirement, or a right, this stops further conversation about the interest. It should come as no surprise that people will lose confidence in an institution that does so.

People will call out such behaviour as nonsense if it stops conversations about human interests inappropriately. And they will call it out as nonsense on stilts if the excuse for stopping the conversation is simply that the human interest has been designated as a human right.

It is still possible, however, to rescue human rights in Australia from being condemned as nonsense on stilts. This is possible if the institutions of law stick to their mandate for stopping conversations about rights, and institutions of politics are reformed so as to stimulate conversations about human interests, rather than trying to stop conversations about human rights.

The debate in 2017 surrounding the survey about changing the definition of marriage gave rise to heated exchanges about whether the demands of non-discrimination can be reconciled with those of religious freedom. Advocates of non-discrimination and religious freedom each claimed that they were the defenders of a human right. There is no doubt that many people have an interest in non-discrimination and many others in religious freedom. To designate either of these as a human right is, however, to end conversation about that interest. So if they are both deemed to be human rights, no conversation is possible about either of them. This is the worst possible political outcome. What is required in Australia are frank conversations about the interests and needs that underpin calls for non-discrimination and the interests and needs that underpin calls for religious freedom. This is a matter of politics. It is a matter of working out how, given the particular circumstances of Australian society, we can best accommodate the particular needs and interests that underpin each of these demands. To recognise them as human rights will only frustrate the possibility of such conversation. What is needed is a parliamentary committee system that facilitates conversation about accommodating these human needs in a way that is of a piece with Australian society, and a commission that can conduct conversations in order to resolve disputes when complaints are made that a person's human interests have been undermined.

Our life in common requires us to take seriously one another's deepest interests, but we allow our finer feelings for our fellow human beings to lead us into stopping conversations about human interests under the guise of protecting human rights at our peril.

We need politics in the form of serious conversations about human interests, rather than the nonsense on stilts of rights discourse, to make our way out of the long grass of human rights.

# Where the light gets in

Catherine Renshaw

Leonard Cohen did not like explaining his music. Nonetheless, in 1992 he made a rare comment about his song "Anthem", from which comes the well-known line: "There is a crack, a crack in everything; That's how the light gets in." What Cohen said was:

> This is not the place where you make things perfect, neither in your marriage, nor in your work, nor anything, nor your love of God, nor your love of family or country. The thing is imperfect. And worse, there is a crack in everything that you can put together: Physical objects, mental objects, constructions of any kind. But that's where the light gets in, and that's where the resurrection is and that's where the return, that's where the repentance is. It is with the confrontation, with the brokenness of things.[1]

Human rights are not a perfect body of philosophical principles, social understandings, or legal practices. Nonetheless human rights and their accompanying institutions are, in our contemporary world, one of those places where the light gets in.

One of the reasons why human rights need rescuing is because the last decade has seen the publication, by eminent writers, of books with chilling titles: *The Twilight of Human Rights*; *Endtimes of Human Rights*; *Human Rights—the Last Utopia*.[2] Many scholars seem to think that the age of human rights is over. Observers might agree. The global human rights system exists without judicial oversight, mechanisms for enforcement or sanctions for non-compliance. It functions by setting standards, which are then invoked (by domestic and international non-governmental organisations, members of civil society, political oppositions, the international community) to persuade, shame or coerce states into compliance.[3] The problems are many. Change is very slow. Many states (both predatory and decent) are resistant to influence. In circumstances of exception (civil conflict, war, political crisis) when human rights are most vulnerable to abuse, the system is least effective.[4]

The practical failures and contradictions of international human rights law are underpinned by long-standing concerns about the philosophical foundations of human rights. There are many and varied theoretical explanations for the source and substance of human rights, but none attract universal acceptance or are completely convincing.[5] The traditional account of human rights is based on a particular moral conception of the human person which tells us, in short, that humans are distinguished (from animals, for example) by having a capacity for practical reason, which leads us to value certain things (such as freedom, agency, autonomy, the ability to make a good life for ourselves) and that because we value these things we have a right to them.[6] This account has been widely criticised.[7] It cannot tell us with certainty what things should count as rights, nor explain where the boundary between rights and goods lies, or why it should be in one place and not another. It cannot explain how it is that human rights are 'universal' rather than historically specific and temporally constrained to the circumstances of particular times.

In textbooks on human rights, discussion of theory is often replaced by historical accounts that present human rights in one of two ways. The first is as a logically continuous progression, beginning in Ancient Greece, evolving in the hands of the policy-makers of the Roman Empire, then moving through the natural rights theorists to the turning-point moments of the French and American Revolutions.[8] Alternatively, it is presented in a way that some scholars have described as the 'Big Bang Theory' of Human Rights, where the beginning of human rights is marked by the birth of the 1948 Universal Declaration of Human Rights, a document made possible by the horror of the Second World War and the Holocaust, which brought together the human race in a moment of revelation that began the modern human rights movement.[9] Neither of these accounts provides a satisfactory conceptual basis for the contemporary practice of human rights.[10]

In the absence of a convincing philosophical foundation for human rights, proponents of non-Western philosophical traditions reasonably ask why the contemporary practice of *human rights* is the best way of understanding and addressing the challenges of modernity: rather than, say, the religious, moral, or ethical practices of their own cultures.[11] Why *should* human rights discourse be the *lingua franca* of the international community? The legitimacy of the global human rights regime is a particular issue in countries that were subjected to European colonialism.[12] Makau Mutua writes: "as currently constituted and deployed, the human rights movement will ultimately fail because it is perceived as an alien ideology in non-Western societies. The movement does not deeply resonate in the cultural fabrics of non-Western states, except among hypocritical elites steeped in Western ideas."[13]

Human rights lawyers and practitioners, whose work often depends on the rhetorical strength of human rights as "universal, indivisible, interdependent and interrelated,"[14] become very anxious at talk of the theoretical weaknesses of human rights. Focused squarely on bettering the lot of the maligned and marginalized, philosophical discussion is seen at best as a second order concern and at worst as a dangerous distraction. At conferences where academics and human rights practitioners mix, it is remarkable to observe how deeply and passionately practitioners argue that to take away from human rights the rhetorical strength of their traditional foundation—the belief that rights are something all human beings are simply endowed with—undercuts the entire human rights movement and does a disservice to millions of oppressed people who cling to the belief that there is a universal yardstick against which the actions of their oppressors will be measured. Many practitioners seem to side with Richard Rorty, who argues that it does not really matter that human rights are without foundation, as long as they are doing some good.[15] Thomas Nagel suggests that the flagrant violation of the most basic human rights should not be reduced to a philosophical conundrum:

> The maintenance of power by the torture and execution of political dissidents or religious minorities, denial of civil rights to women, total censorship, and so forth demand denunciation and practical opposition, not theoretical discussion. One could be pardoned for thinking that the philosophical interest of an issue is inversely proportional to its real-life significance.[16]

Despite its lack of solid philosophical foundations, Western origins and enlightenment heritage, the Universal Declaration of Human Rights has guided struggles for the emancipation of colonised peoples, women, and religious minorities in developed and developing states. All these groups have invoked the idea that they are born free and equal in dignity and rights, without cavilling about the metaphysical basis for their claim. A variety of arguments are offered to support the universalism of human rights. One argument is that although human rights arose in the West, in particular socio-political conditions associated with modernity, *all* nations are now experiencing these same conditions (the rise of a powerful and intrusive nation state; industrialization; state-sponsored assaults on liberties) and so all nations now need human rights; human rights are relevant to all.[17] Another argument is that in *all* cultures there is respect for a common core of values that provides a platform for grounding a universal morality that is now reflected in the discourse of international human rights.[18] Thomas Nagel, for example, believes that certain rights constitute a "core of inviolability" to which no cost-benefit analysis applies, and that some things are wrong regardless of culture or circumstance (for example, the maintenance of power by the torture and execution of public dissidents or religious minorities, denial of civil rights to women, total censorship).[19] Charles Taylor names genocide, murder, torture and slavery as things that all cultures have condemned.[20] Bernard Williams also recognises some acts as "abuses of power that almost everyone everywhere has been in a position to recognise"[21] and John Rawls identifies certain rights as "human rights proper", which cannot be rejected as particularly liberal or special to the Western tradition.[22] For most who have written in this vein, the list of core, inter-culturally valid rights are the same as the non-derogable rights listed in the International Covenant on Civil and Political Rights: the right to life; freedom from torture, slavery, arbitrary arrest and imprisonment; recognition before the law; and freedom of thought, conscience and religion.[23]

Others have sought to derive a deep core value which has been common to every system of belief subscribed to at all times by all peoples.[24] Respect for 'human dignity' is often the value identified. Within the Confucian tradition, for example, some have pointed to the fact that although 'human rights' do not exist as a concept in Confucian thought,[25] one can find in the works of Confucius and Mencius a focus on humanity and human dignity in the ideas of *ren* ('human heartedness') and *shu* (comparing in a compassionate manner one's own heart with other hearts) which is compatible with the philosophy of contemporary international human rights.[26] Onuma Yasuaki calls such theories a "theory of universal origin", a way for intellectuals and human right advocates in diverse societies to argue: "look, human rights are not alien. They are already in *our* religion (culture, customs, etc.)"[27]

Theories of universal origin are an attempt to show empirically what cannot be proven philosophically: that human rights are innate and universal. But from an empirical perspective, it is difficult to argue that even very basic rights are universal: that is, that they have been accepted, at all times, by all cultures.[28] Values assumed to be cross-culturally valid because they are found in every culture are often either very vague or very meagre.[29] Attempts to give meaning to the concept of 'dignity', for example, are often of limited practical utility. In Raimon Pannikar's conception of the caste system, dignity might derive from one's role in a social order, and one's rights might be the rights that attach to a person as ruler, wife, mother, or street-sweeper. In such an order, there is manifest dignity in a wife's fulfilment of *sati* after the death of her husband. But Western observers would find it difficult to see how in these circumstances the wife could be said to possess freedom and equality in the same way that her husband does. Clearly if human rights are broadly understood and cultures are sympathetically interpreted, then different cultures are capable of supporting a doctrine of human rights. The question is; Why should they? Why should a moral community be built around an understanding of human beings as rational, and free and equal? It might be the case that norms of freedom and equality do in fact best protect those things that some societies hold most dear. Strong arguments have been made about the instrumental value of individual freedoms in terms of the large contribution to the common good made by protection and promotion of these rights.[30] But this cannot just be assumed.

The difficulty with theories of universal origin is that they set out to prove a pre-determined position, which is that human rights *are* indeed universal. It remains the case that in much of the world, the language of human rights is a pastiche, covering deeper and more resonant cultural traditions that do not, in fact, always lead in the same direction as international human rights law. Human rights are not inter-culturally self-evident. This does not mean that they do not exist in non-Western cultures. It simply means that the doctrine of human rights needs to justify itself, particularly when it is placed in juxtaposition with other powerful cultures and traditions. Panikkar explains this point elegantly from the perspective of Hinduism. Panikkar's answer to the question of whether human rights are universal is 'yes', human rights are universal from the vantage point of modern

Western culture. But they are not universal from the vantage points of other cultures. Human rights are, according to Panikkar, just one window through which one particular culture envisages a just human order for its individuals; other cultures have other windows. Panikkar suggests that instead of smashing the windows and making of the many portals "a single gaping aperture", we should instead "enlarge the viewpoints as much as possible and, most of all, make people aware that there are, and have to be, a plurality of windows."[31]

In recent years, an alternative to both the natural law theory of human rights and the theory of universal origin has been proposed. Known as the "political conception of human rights,"[32] its central feature is that it eschews metaphysical questioning and looks to the existing discourse and practice of human rights, seeking to clarify the understandings of human rights with respect to its own aims and purposes. It is above all a practical perspective, with a pedigree that can be traced to the drafting of the Universal Declaration of Human Rights itself. In 1948, the conclusion to long and acrimonious disputes about the philosophical basis of human rights was simply to adopt what Jacques Maritain described as a "practical viewpoint and concern ourselves no longer with seeking the basis and philosophic significance of human rights but only their statement and enumeration."[33] According to Maritain, the point of developing a conception of human rights, capable of being shared by adherents to different traditions, was to create agreement "not on the basis of common speculative ideas, but on common practical ideas, not on the affirmation of one and the same conception of the world, of man, and of knowledge, but on the affirmation of a single body of beliefs for guidance on action."[34] Michael Ignatieff, a prominent proponent of political conceptions of human rights, argues for an understanding of human rights that emphasises their inherently political nature. Statements of human rights are not an attempt to proclaim an ultimate truth; they are instead a common framework for deliberation among parties who might otherwise disagree. They are not 'moral trumps' above politics, but a common ground for argument and debate about political conflicts.

In contemporary moral philosophy, the political conception of human rights takes various forms. But at its core are three central concepts. The first concerns the nature of the interests protected by the practice of human rights. The interests are *urgent individual interests* which are vulnerable under typical conditions of life in a modern world order comprised of states.[35] These urgent interests are those things that give individuals the opportunity to participate as members in political society. Charles Beitz, employing Rawls's ideas of 'reasonable agreement' and 'overlapping consensus', argues that these interests are ones that most of us would recognise as important in a wide range of lives in contemporary society.[36] They provide, in Baynes's words: "a thin conception of moral reciprocity: the idea that others should be protected from the pain and humiliation that we could not imagine having inflicted on ourselves."[37] Secondly, rights are held against the state and its institutions; they are not just innately 'held.'[38] Finally, human rights are 'political' in the sense that their denial gives rise to a political claim for recognition.[39] Human rights emerge through political action (and speech) that asserts the existence of rights that are not presently recognised.[40] The 'practice' of human rights, then, is the process by which political institutions and communities are challenged and then forced to either justify suppression and exclusion or to become more inclusive and egalitarian. The archetypal example of this might be Rosa Parks refusing to give up her seat to a white man on a bus in Montgomery, Alabama, in 1955. Parks was making two simultaneous claims: (1) that she was equal; and (2) that her equality was denied. Her act was a demonstration that she possessed the equality that was not recognised.

From this perspective, the practice of human rights is not an exercise in finding consensus about the character and application of rights. It is precisely the opposite. The practice of human rights means paying attention to dissensus concerning the meaning, application and extension of rights: and experimental activation by those to whom rights could (but do not yet) apply. One point that arises from this conception of human rights is that the list of what human rights—these urgent interests—*are* is not definite or settled. It is subject to revision or extension. This is the point I would like to take up in this introductory essay, because it addresses one of the major criticisms of human rights, which is that the list of human rights has expanded uncontrollably to include things which those who drafted the Universal Declaration of Human Rights would not have viewed as rights, such as the right of couples of the same sex to marry one another.

In Australia, the denial of same-sex marriage ended in 2017 with the passage of the *Marriage Amendment (Definition and Religious Freedoms) Act*. The Act was the culmination of a passionately debated contest between those who, on the one hand, viewed same sex marriage as an issue of equality and opponents who, on the other hand, viewed the traditional form of marriage as the natural order of things and deviations from it as a dangerous concession to a post-modernist fad. The case against same sex marriage was that heteronormative relationships as the basis of marriage were fundamental to society's survival and that society has a right to ensure its survival. The case was put succinctly by Prime Minister John Howard:

> Traditional marriage is one of the bedrock institutions of our society. . . . Marriage, as we understand it in our society, is about children, having children, raising them, providing for the survival of the species and I think if the same status is given in our society to gay unions as are given to traditional marriage we will weaken that bedrock institution.[41]

The case against same sex marriage was supported by Australian religious leaders such as Dr Jensen, the Anglican Archbishop of Sydney:

> Ensuring public honour of same-sex relationships by calling them marriages is an abuse of marriage itself . . . It imposes, through social

engineering, a newly minted concept of marriage on a community that understands it in quite another way.[42]

The demand from gay and lesbian Australians was framed as a demand for justice conceived as equality of respect. Raimond Gaita put it this way:

> Is it hyperbole to say that when gays and lesbians demand the right to marry, they demand acknowledgment of their full humanity? I believe it is not. Recall my earlier claim that to acknowledge someone as a fellow human being is to see him or her as capable of rising fully, in full responsiveness, to the meaning of the defining facts of the human condition. One of those defining facts is our sexuality and the way it goes deep with us – so deep as to be fundamental to our sense of identity.[43]

The debate about sexual equality rights in Australia was marked—and in many parts of the world continues to be marked—by individual acts that assert the equal moral worth and value of people regardless of sexuality. It need not be said that these individual acts challenging suppression and exclusion are ones of great courage. In Britain during the 1950s, when homosexual conduct was a criminal offence, Peter Wildeblood (together with Lord Montagu and Michael PittRivers) was charged and convicted with committing acts of homosexual indecency. In court, Peter Wildeblood described his sexuality in these terms:

> I am no more proud of my condition than I would be of having a glass eye or a hare lip. On the other hand, I am no more ashamed of it than I would be of being colour-blind or of writing with my left hand . . . I am attracted towards men in the way in which most men are attracted towards women. I am aware that many people, luckier than myself, will read this statement with incredulity and perhaps with derision; but it is the simple truth. I know that it cannot ever be entirely accepted by the rest of the community and I do not ask that it should . . . If it were possible for me to become like them I should do so.[44]

In his autobiography, Wildeblood describes his reasons for openly declaring his sexuality:

> I could see what I must do. I would be the first homosexual to tell what it felt like to be an exile in one's own country. I might destroy myself, but perhaps I could help others.[45]

From within the framework of a political conception of human rights, assessing a human rights claim for sexual equality involves a normative assessment of the value and risk inherent in recognising the claim. It requires that we form an objective, rational view of our society, its cohesiveness, strengths and weaknesses, and the legitimate threat society might face from the challenge to its existing structure and norms.

The question of what threatens the survival of society was addressed in 1963, in what was to become a famous exchange between Professor H. L. A. Hart and Lord Devlin on the subject of public morality and the criminalisation of homosexuality, prostitution, and pornography. Lord Devlin, responding to the Wolfenden Report, which argued for the decriminalisation of homosexuality, claimed that a degree of moral conformity was essential to society, and that every society has a right to preserve its own existence by insisting on some such conformity – through the mechanism of the criminal law if necessary. Lord Devlin acknowledged that individual freedom was important, and that a society must be cautious about concluding that a practice is profoundly immoral to the extent that it forbids it.[46] Nonetheless, his view was that when public feeling in relation to an issue rises to the level of "intolerance, indignation and disgust," if the broad popular feeling is genuinely that a particular practice is an abominable vice, then society's right to eradicate that practice cannot be denied.[47]

Professor Hart's response was that society was not as fragile as Lord Devlin imagined it to be, and that Lord Devlin offered no evidence to support his claim that the tolerance of individuals practices which ran against the moral grain of society jeopardized society's survival. He suggested that Lord Devlin was adopting a definition of society that was highly artificial—as a particular complex of moral ideas and attitudes which its members happen to hold at a particular moment in time. Why, (argued Professor Hart), should such a moral status quo have the right to preserve its precarious existence by force? In his answer to Professor Hart, Lord Devlin argued his claim was not that *any* deviation from a society's shared morality threatened its existence, merely that it was possible to conceive of some activities so morally at odds with societal moral consensus that they *could* threaten the existence of society, and that there should be no constitutional barrier to assessing this risk and criminalising these activities.

The critical issue is how this risk should be assessed: how do we know when the danger presented to society by a particular practice is sufficiently clear and present to justify prohibition?[48] Some of the difficulties surrounding this question were addressed by Ronald Dworkin in an article published in the *Yale Law Journal* in 1966.[49] In that article, Dworkin considered whether public condemnation, in and of itself, should be sufficient to justify making an act a crime, and whether if public condemnation was *not* sufficient, what more might be needed. He also wondered whether there must be some demonstration of present harm to particular persons directly affected by the practice in question, or whether it might be sufficient to show some effect on social customs and institutions which alters the social environment, and thus affects all members of society indirectly. Applying these questions to Lord Devlin's argument that society's abhorrence of homosexuality justified its prohibition, Dworkin noted that Lord Devlin offered no evidence that homosexuality presents any danger at all to society's existence, beyond the naked claim that all "deviations from a society's shared morality . . . are capable in their nature of threatening the existence of society" and so "cannot be put beyond the law." Dworkin concludes that Lord Devlin simply *believed* that the ordinary man in the street thought that homosexuality "was a vice so abominable that its mere presence is an offence"[50] and that society was therefore justified in outlawing it, leaving homosexuals to choose, in Dworkin's words, "between the miseries of frustration and persecution."[51]

Dworkin argues strongly that public condemnation by itself ought not to be enough to justify restricting the liberties of individuals. This is because public feeling might not be based on good reasons, but might instead be based on prejudices, personal aversions and rationalizations, which do not by themselves justify restricting important individual freedoms. In Dworkin's view, legislators have a responsibility to test claims about the existence of a moral consensus, by studying the community's reactions to practices, participating in and encouraging public debate, and studying the views contained in editorial columns, the speeches of colleagues, the testimony of interested groups, and the view of constituents. These arguments and positions must be sifted in order to determine which are prejudices or rationalizations, and which represent a genuine reasoned moral consensus. Dworkin was quite sure that Lord Devlin held an incorrect view about the moral consensus on homosexuality in Britain in the 1960's: "what is shocking and wrong is not his [Lord Devlin's] idea that the community's morality counts, but his idea of what counts as the community's morality."

Institutions and processes designed to promote and protect human rights have a crucial role to play in assisting us to make normative assessments about the value or danger of recognising or rejecting different rights claims. They also play an essential part in fostering the debate and discussion that is necessary to make reasoned decisions about where the balance should lie between individual liberty and social cohesion. The Australian Human Rights Commission, for example, is a federal statutory body with a mandate to foster education and public awareness about human rights, investigate discrimination and human rights complaints, promote human rights compliance and engage in policy and legislative development. During the same sex marriage debate, the Commission drew attention to research which indicated that discrimination, social exclusion and homophobia contributed to negative health outcomes and the Commission pointed to reports that showed how removing legislative discrimination to recognise marriage for all couples could help reduce marginalisation and promote a stronger and more accepting society. Marriage equality was not held up by the Commission as a 'right' intended to trump all discourse. Instead, the issue was framed as an invitation to debate. What was the compelling social purpose in restricting marriage to couples of different sexes? Was there a rational connection between this limitation and a strong, stable and cohesive society? Does the evidence tell us that a restrictive definition of marriage is reasonable and necessary, to achieve a legitimate social goal? Ultimately, the conservative position on same-sex marriage failed because its proponents could not convince enough Australians that recognising equality in relation to marriage was the danger they claimed it to be.

One important conclusion that follows from accepting a political conception of human rights as the most appropriate way of understanding the contemporary practice of human rights is attention to the role and importance of duties. In his (very brief) contribution to the UNESCO Committee on the Drafting of the Universal Declaration of Human Rights, Mahatma Gandhi suggested that instead of a list of rights, it might be better for the Committee to "define the duties of every Man and Woman and correlate every right to some corresponding duty to be first performed. Every other right can be shown to be a usurpation hardly worth fighting for." Article 29(1) of the Universal Declaration of Human Rights, states that: "Everyone has duties to the community in which alone the free and full development of his personality is possible."[52] Regional human rights instruments such as the American Declaration of the Rights and Duties of Man,[53] the American Convention on Human Rights,[54] the African Charter on Human and Peoples' Rights[55] also contain references to duties; and duties in the form of 'responsibilities' is present in Australian state based human rights instruments such as the Victorian Charter or Rights and Responsibilities. Indeed nearly all of the human rights instruments created since World War II have provided express or implied recognition of duties. Writing in the *Harvard Human Rights Journal* twenty years ago, Jordan J. Paust advised a shift from theoretical inquiries about whether duties existed in international human rights law, to questions about what sorts of duty correspond to what sorts of rights in what contexts, how competing rights should be accommodated, and how these ultimately affect public responsibility.[56]

Despite their prominence in international human rights instruments, duties have historically been treated cautiously by human rights lawyers. Ben Saul, for example, in his critique of the 1997 Draft Declaration of Human Responsibilities, created by the Inter-Action Council, argues that:

(1) duties cannot be defined with sufficient clarity and precision to make them useful legal concepts;

(2) duties involve subtle and particularistic matters of custom and lore, better suited to local systems of morality rather than codification at the international level;

(3) historically, the concept of human duties has proven open to abuse and manipulation.[57]

Yash Ghai notes that in the hands of some governments, the concept of duty becomes a justification for, as well as an instrument of, authoritarianism.[58] Ghai points out that in societies where ideas of duty predominate "the system becomes reminiscent of feudalism with persons at the top of the hierarchy having rights and those at the lower reaches, duties."[59] He notes that the fulfilment of duties frequently betokens social, economic, or political subordination, and tends towards conservatism and the perpetuation of inequalities. The emphasis on duties which permeates the policies and rhetoric of some political leaders essentialises citizens as people who are obedient and devoted to the community; and civic and national virtue as demanding an orientation away from 'individualistic' demands.[60] In these circumstances the political logic following from an emphasis on duty is a constraint of civil and political rights in the name of order, harmony and control. There is often a clear strand of utilitarian thinking in this kind of philosophy about duties: an idea that individual rights might justifiably be 'traded-off' against a greater good.[61]

There are several respects in which duties play a role in political conceptions of human rights. Joseph Raz employs the notion of duties to identify whether something is a right at all. Raz argues that a person has a right if some aspect of her wellbeing (some 'interest') is sufficiently important to justify holding another person or persons to be under a duty to respect and fulfil that right. A's right to marry whomever she chooses, for example, is sufficiently important from a moral point of view to justify holding the state under a duty not to restrict A in this regard.[62] Amartya Sen employs the notion of duties as part of the process necessary to determine how we can prevent the human rights of others from being violated or aid their enjoyment of rights. For Sen, all of us have a basic general obligation (a duty) to engage in an act of deliberative reasoning in order to work out what should be done, given the parameters of a particular case.[63] Thomas Pogge has offered a more specific and demanding idea of duty, arguing that every person has a duty not to cooperate in imposing an unjust institutional scheme upon others, one that might violate their rights in indirect ways, and that continued participation in an unjust institutional scheme, triggers obligations to promote feasible reforms of this scheme.[64]

At a fundamental level, the concept of duty in political conceptions of human rights is linked to the notion of justification. In her discussion on the drafting of the Universal Declaration of Human Rights, Mary Ann Glendon comments in relation to Article 29, the 'duties' article, that the duties are meant to apply in "a certain kind of community, where the free and full development of [the individual's] personality is possible."[65] The Declaration does actually not say this. The Declaration states that it is "the community alone in which the free and full development of his personality is possible" and this is why the individual owes the community duties. But Glendon is trying to make the point that we cannot owe duties to communities in which we are not free and equal members, in which our views about balancing rights, and the relationship between rights and duties, are ignored or subjugated.

In Kantian terms, to be an 'end' and not a 'means' of others is to be able to demand justification for the continuing existence of laws, institutions or power relations that are in your view unjust. There is a duty—which often requires a significant amount of courage to exercise—to demand reasons for the actions that affect one. The corresponding duty on the part of those who control and maintain laws, institutions and power relations is to provide reasons that are objective and rational. This is the "normative deep grammar of social protests and struggles in which concrete demands for justification are associated with the language of rights."[66] Through this process there is what the German legal philosopher Rainer Forst describes as a dynamic logic of 'moral modernization' in which there are increasing demands for explanations about the structure of existing orders and ever more constructive justifications given to those affected by them. It is a process that ends in one of three ways: by the extension of rights and liberties to those negatively affected by the existing order; by the provision of sufficient justification; or by the use of power and force.

It should be clear from what I have written so far that the gravest danger to human rights is constraint on deliberative democracy—limitations on discourse and debate about the conditions under which people can participate in shaping the kind of society in which they live. Decisions that affect people's lives—particularly the deepest and most personal aspects of people's lives—must be transparent, fair, broad, participatory, inclusive and wide-ranging, and the marginalised and vulnerable, who after all are the primary intended beneficiaries of human rights, must be able to participate. Institutions such as the Australian Human Rights Commission have a critical role to play in fostering debate and creating the conditions for consensus in circumstances of reasonable disagreement. Other opinions are also relevant:

the views of religious leaders and philosophers are relevant to the scope and content of rights in a just and inclusive society, as well as the views of legal experts and politicians, and the views of ordinary people—reflected in public forums and social media. Upholding and reinforcing the ideal of deliberative democracy, which is in modern times understood as a central element of the legitimacy of law (including human rights law) is the ultimate answer to the question of how to rescue human rights.

**RESPONDING TO DAMIEN FREEMAN AND CATHERINE RENSHAW**

# 1. The use and usefulness of rights in our parliament

Terri Butler

In December 2017, after a long campaign for change, and after several failed attempts, the Australian Parliament legislated to amend the Marriage Act, to provide that 'marriage' means the union of two people to the exclusion of all others, voluntarily entered into for life.

Advocates for marriage equality had long advocated for the change, on grounds including, prominently, human rights and non-discrimination principles. Others had advocated against making the change, arguing on the basis of conservative values, religious beliefs, and also human rights. The issue had been ventilated at party conferences, in the opinion pages of the press, and in community events. Previous private members' bills had been tabled; in 2012, a vote had been held, unsuccessfully, in the House of Representatives. The human rights recognised in the treaties and conventions to which Australia is a party had been materially the same throughout that time. What then, was the extent to which the existence of human rights in international instruments contributed to the change in our domestic marriage laws in 2017?

There were many influences upon the Parliament's decision to change the law. That is another way of saying that there were many influences upon the votes cast by Members and Senators in the course of changing the law. Some of those influences were more visible and obvious than others. There was fierce lobbying, public campaigning, appeals to conscience and morality (on both sides of the argument), arguments based on social benefit (the promotion of better mental health through inclusion, for example), and pressure being brought to bear by party members and leaders. There were also ancillary considerations, such as whether adopting a particular stance, or voting a particular way on a procedural question to bring the substantive matter on for debate, would be, or would be portrayed as being, disloyal to one's values, party, or constituencies. These considerations affected both procedural when and how the matter could be debated and substantive decision-making, with the former, as always, affecting the latter in practical ways. (Specifically, the decision as to whether to cross the floor, taking into account loyalty and unity rather than one's view on the merits of the bill itself, arguably prevented a vote from being held much earlier than it ultimately was.)

In describing some of the many influences that affected the decision collectively made by Members and Senators (and their Queen), it should be noted that parliamentarians are not homogenous: they hold differing beliefs and perspectives, and they find different things persuasive. Even parliamentarians who agree as to the most desirable outcome may have reached the conclusion by different routes. It seems that amongst those who wished for the marriage amendment bill to be passed, compatibility with human rights was an important consideration, but not the only consideration. Different parliamentarians would have afforded compatibility with human rights generally, as well as compatibility with specific human rights, different weights in their decision-making. In understanding the effect that rights-based analyses may have had on decision-making, it is useful to consider the specific attempts that were made, in the course of this issue, to evaluate the proposed marriage law amendments in the context of human rights.

Australia has ratified several international instruments that set out human rights.[1] Australia was not legally compelled to sign or ratify any of those instruments; they were entered into voluntarily. Making that assertion does not ignore that moral and political suasion, both domestic and international, can be brought to bear upon governments to enter into covenants. The point being made is that our nation, through its government, decided to take on the obligations inherent in becoming a party to an international instrument, including to adhere to and act consistently with those rights set out in it. It is those rights that are being considered here.

In considering those rights I am not oblivious to criticism of rights-based arguments that have been made over many decades, many of which are averted to in Catherine Renshaw's contribution to this volume. I acknowledge the valid concerns of those who consider rights to be of benefit only to those with the power to enforce them, or who have the good fortune of being the beneficiary of others who have both the power and the inclination to enforce rights in their favour. I also acknowledge other concerns such as those as to whether the universalist approach to human rights is at best ignorant and at worst cultural imperialism. Some say rights are too individualistic, some (such as Damien Freeman, in this volume), are of the view that the term 'right' has been stretched too far, and that some of the (economic, social, and cultural) rights are not really rights at all but interests. The approach of using human rights as a framework for evaluation of proposed laws is far from perfect. Deliberately considering human rights while making domestic laws nonetheless remains an important means by which to protect or at least promote the interests of the public as a whole, of individuals, or of those susceptible to oppression, depending on the circumstances.

Considering the rights set out in international instruments requires no statement about the source of those rights. This approach is consistent with the political conception of human rights that Renshaw discusses elsewhere in this volume. It does not matter, for the purpose of analysing a proposed law using a framework of recognised human rights, whether those rights pre-existed the international instruments because they are 'natural' rights derived from the nature of people, or were handed down from God, or came into existence only when the international instrument itself was first signed. It does not matter for present purposes whether they can or should be said to be universal, or whether they are rights that reflect particular cultural values or the preoccupations of persons with a particular ideology. It does not matter whether the justification for the existence of rights per se is rationality or sentimentality. It is a matter of fact that these instruments exist, that Australia has deliberately and, at law, at least, freely signed and ratified them, and that they describe certain rights that they say that all people have. In other words, they set out human rights that apply in Australia because our nation has agreed that they do, and no other reason is needed to establish the application of those rights to proposed domestic laws.

Human rights were at the heart of a Senate select committee report into the government's exposure draft of a bill to amend the Marriage Act.[2] Human rights were also considered in the ordinary processes of the parliament. Those are discussed below, but for now it suffices to say that the usual rights-analysis processes, undertaken for each bill, provided useful information, but the select committee was more influential. Its character as a specially-constituted inquiry with representation from across party lines, willing to work from a government-produced exposure draft bill, and with the goodwill and determination needed to produce a unanimous report, gave the committee's work significant weight. The select committee described at length the human rights that would be 'engaged' by the bill, and then discussed in detail how those rights might be 'balanced'. This report was an input into the political decision-making of the parliament, in relation to proposals to change the law of marriage. Neither it nor the usual human rights analyses were capable, though, of binding the parliament to make a particular decision or adopt a particular amendment. Such analysis is informative and persuasive but not determinative.

The subsequent national postal survey was another input into the parliament's decision-making. Undertaking a national survey did not fit with a human rights approach to changing the marriage law. It was not consistent with an argument that parliament should, or, even more strongly, was obliged to, change the law of marriage as the best means of 'balancing' human rights that applied through the voluntary ratification of international treaties. Advocates during the postal survey campaign may well have argued that a 'yes' vote was appropriate to give effect to human rights, but the survey itself told the parliament nothing about what human rights existed or what rights our nation had promised to uphold. The survey told the parliament only whether the Australian people at the time supported a change to the law. The basis on which this public opinion had been formed is and was unknowable.

At the time of the survey, former High Court Justice Michael Kirby described the inconsistency between a rights-based approach and the survey process:[3]

> The objection to having a person's legal equality determined by a vote of any kind, outside the Parliament, is obvious. You don't allow people's fundamental human rights or their fundamental legal rights to be determined by the votes of a majority of other people. That is simply self-evident.

Not only was the survey inconsistent with a rights-based approach to marriage equality; if the outcome had been different, and a majority of the people had voted 'no', the existence of the survey would have been a consideration in support of oppression of the minority and of failing to give effect to their human rights. In such a circumstance, the parliament would have had to choose between giving best effect to balancing human rights or giving effect to public opinion and sentiment. Parliamentarians would have been and were answerable for their decisions at the ballot-box. This goes to the heart of what it means to be a good parliamentarian, as Edmund Burke identified centuries ago: the obligation to exercise judgement in the face of opinion.[4]

The modern international human rights framework, and especially meaningful evaluation of how rights can be given practical effect, can assist a parliamentarian in exercising judgement, albeit that this framework is far from the only source of assistance in that regard.

As stated above, in collectively deciding to change the law, parliamentarians had before them a range of inputs into their decision-making, some of which were in conflict. We can discern, from the Senate select committee's report, that the human rights framework is sufficiently influential to be the main framework through which the proposed bill was evaluated.

The focus on human rights by the select committee in the marriage equality example is perhaps unsurprising given that the evaluation of the interaction between proposed laws and human rights is part of the parliament's ordinary day-to-day work. As mentioned, there are standard processes of the parliament that evaluate bills and other instruments against human rights. The *Human Rights (Parliamentary Scrutiny) Act 2011* sets out two mechanisms by which such evaluations occur: a requirement that a bill's proponent produce a statement of compatibility with human rights, and the establishment of a joint standing committee to evaluate proposed laws' compatibility with human rights. In both cases, by explicit statutory requirement, the human rights under consideration are specifically those set out in the international instruments referred to above.

In addition, there is, established under the Senate standing orders, a committee of the Senate which has the task of scrutinising bills with regard to whether they trespass unduly on personal rights and liberties, and with regard to other similar issues.[5] These are traditional civil and political rights; Bentham would have approved of the use of the term 'unduly' given he considered the imprescriptability of rights to be nonsense on stilts.

So too, the processes established under the Human Rights (Parliamentary Scrutiny) Act that require evaluation of the compatibility of proposed legislation with human rights create opportunities to inform rather than constrain parliamentary decision-making. Therefore, the legislation establishing them implicitly recognises that rights are more akin to claims than trumps.

Freeman has cited criticism from one of my colleagues, Julian Leeser MP, of one of the mechanisms provided for under the Human Rights (Parliamentary Scrutiny) Act, specifically, the creation of the Parliamentary Joint Committee on Human Rights. The criticisms appear to go to: (a) whether the committee is tacitly controlled by bureaucrats rather than elected representatives; (b) the suite of rights against which the committee evaluates bills; (c) the form of reports going to evaluation and comparative analysis with the rights themselves, rather than going to questions of judgement, justification, and discretion as to the extent to which the parliament should curtail rights; and (d) whether the reports are quasi-constitutional limitations on legislative power, or, at least, tend to shut down debate rather than facilitate it. Freeman agrees with Leeser that this particular committee process treats what are more accurately described as human interests as if they were human rights (and therefore trumps that prevent discussion).

As to the first matter, the committee's members are Members and Senators, and its powers are as determined by resolution of both Houses of Parliament. The resolution as most recently made provides for broad powers.[6] Neither the statute nor the resolution allows for the will of the committee to be overborne by unelected secretariat staff. The committee takes a technical and non-partisan approach by convention. At law, therefore, it is a matter for the committee whether to take the advice of its advisors; any constraints upon it to do so are political, not legal. The extent to which parliamentarians are 'free' in a political sense to accept or refuse advice in our democracy at any given time is a much broader question. It is related to issues such as the extent to which the citizenry has confidence in democracy, and the extent to which the society tends towards favouring technocratic decision-making, among many others. Parliamentarians' propensity to consider themselves constrained, politically, by advice is affected by these considerations; it is also affected by the personal attributes (such as skill, courage, and experience) of individual parliamentarians. In a committee setting there are procedures available to ensure that advice given is kept confidential, along with confidentiality requirements in respect of draft reports, draft minutes, and the like, as well as the capacity to hold meetings in camera. All of these arrangements lessen the likelihood of political constraint in the sense referred to above, as they assist in ensuring that the outputs of committees are genuinely the views of the democratically elected parliamentarians, aggregated into unanimous reports if possible, and expressed as dissents or additional comments, if not.

The second matter goes to questions of whether all rights are equal, whether some are more important than others, and which rights ought to be included in the human rights framework against which the committee analyses bills. Any reading of the legislation shows that the parliament intended that the committee analyse bills against the framework of the international human rights instruments to which Australia is a party. The instruments are specified in the Act; they are those instruments listed above.

Human rights cannot all be absolutes, particularly because, subject to the prevailing circumstances, rights may and do come into conflict. There is not, and cannot be, a comprehensive ranking of every single right from most to least important; albeit rights *can* be grouped (into absolute rights, into non-derogable rights, as occurs in the International Covenant on Civil and Political Rights). It is a matter for democratic processes to determine as between competing rights or decide that abrogation of a (non-absolute) right or rights is justified in the circumstances. For example, a legislature might decide that a right to freedom of speech should be limited to protect property rights by legislating against passing-off or misleading or deceptive conduct. At the same time, a lack of incursion into a right might tell us very little about the moral basis for legislation; it might be that though a potential law does not breach a right, it does little or nothing to give effect to it. For example, a domestic law asserting a social, economic, or cultural right, such as the right to housing, might be considered lacking if it provides for no practical means of giving effect to that right.

Similarly, parliamentarians' opinions about which rights are important and worthy of consideration may differ. One might be more attentive to individual civil and political rights; another, to economic, social, and cultural rights. None should have the right to decide, unilaterally, which rights matter enough to be considered. That is properly a matter for the parliament as a whole. The parliament has, by the 2011 Act, decided that the committee should consider all of the rights set out in the international instruments named in the Act. That can be changed through legislative amendment if the parliament is so persuaded. However, including all of the rights that are contained in the international instruments seems to be a well-founded approach. Deciding that only some of the rights—or rights set out in only some of the international instruments—are worthy of being included in the technical analysis would seem fraught.

The third matter goes to the type of reports the committee produces. It is clear that an evaluation of whether a bill offends against, curtails, or otherwise restricts the exercise of any right set out in an international instrument is a useful but insufficient input for a parliamentarian exercising judgement. A parliamentarian might also want to know what experts, stakeholders, or the community at large thinks about the bill, or what a distributional, utilitarian, feminist, critical race theory, or other analysis would have to say about the bill. Happily, the Parliamentary Joint Committee on Human Rights is not the only means of inquiring into the bill. As mentioned, the proponent is required to provide an explanatory memorandum with a statement of compatibility on human rights. In addition, other formal requirements such as regulatory impact statements, or a Senate inquiry into a bill, or the recommendations of other parliamentary inquiries into similar subject matter, are all likely to be useful and come from different vantage points than a rights-based technical analysis. Similarly, parliamentarians may read advice from the Library, or make their own enquiries to seek differing opinions.

The final point goes to whether a purportedly neutral technical report shuts down debate. Does it position rights as trumps, and act as a quasi-constitutional restraint on parliamentary decision-making? It does not. The recommendations of one committee cannot be determinative, no matter how persuasive they might be; in the final analysis, it is the decision of the parliament that determines the outcome, not the recommendation of any particular committee.

Freeman follows Geuss in arguing that rights are always trumps, and that no discussion can be had when trumps are at play. I respectfully disagree with that proposition when it comes to parliamentary decision-making. My disagreement is founded on the nature of rights, and on the nature of the predominant work of legislatures, which is to make the law, rather than to apply it. As argued elsewhere in this chapter, rights can conflict. In making the law, the legislature is called upon to decide which is to prevail. A later legislature, in different historical circumstances, may come to a different decision. Nations and peoples' views of rights change over time, a point akin to that which Renshaw makes in her contribution to this volume. Accommodating rights into law-making can raise as many questions as answers. The clash of rights is a cause of disagreement and debate. It gives rise to circumstances that demand that parliamentarians exercise their judgement and discretion: the clash of rights forces them to make choices about what the law ought to be.

In the course of their decision-making, parliamentarians are able to express their views about matters of judgement and discretion. Whether a proposed law curtails a right is far from the end of the matter. As described above, there may be very good justifications for the curtailment, and, by the same token, the absence of curtailment may not be sufficient reason to support a bill.

For Bentham, it was the naturalness of rights that was nonsense, and the imprescriptability of them that was nonsense on stilts; those criticisms cannot be fairly made of our parliament. The rights under consideration are not revealed to us, supposedly naturally existing, prior to the creation of the state: they are rights set out in specific international conventions to which we decided to be a party. Save for a very small number of rights within the category of absolute rights, rights are considered to be in need of balancing and of domestic application. That is part of the parliament's ordinary work. There are no stilts here.

It is the balancing that takes judgment. In the case of marriage equality, the balancing was said to be between rights relating to children, marriage, non-discrimination, and religious freedom. None of these rights as claims was uncontroversial. Most if not all of these rights were used in the arguments put by advocates on both sides of the issue. Ultimately, it is up to lawmakers to exercise that judgement. That is why a human rights committee's report cannot be a case of rights as trumps. Like other inputs, it can be considered and debated during the reading of the bill in question. Those debates are conducted, and the decisions are made, in a manner formally unconstrained by the conceptual framework of rights per se, let alone the specific rights recognised within that framework. Providing advice to the parliament as to the extent to which a piece of legislation provides an incursion upon a human right (as articulated internationally and as ratified domestically) does not shut down debate. It ensures debate does not occur in the absence of salient information.

By the same token, deliberative democracy processes involving unelected persons can be an input into parliamentary decision-making. Renshaw sees deliberative democracy as the means by which to 'rescue' human rights. Deliberative democracy is a broad term and can range from individual citizens lobbying parliamentarians, to so-called mini-publics and plebiscites. As is the case with advice from secretariats, and with committee reports, these processes should not be considered determinative, legally or politically. Great care should be taken with the deployment of such processes. Just as Michael Kirby criticized the idea that a majority should decide whether human rights should be afforded to a minority, and just as Burke warned that parliamentarians should not sacrifice their judgement to their electors' opinion, so too should it ultimately be a matter for the elected parliamentarians to determine collectively how our nation's voluntarily acquired obligations to give effect to human rights should be translated into domestic law.

Having regard to the foregoing, rights are useful as a framework, and as a significant consideration in decision-making, but the sovereignty of parliament applies. The fact that laws can be made notwithstanding that they limit, in practical ways, the rights articulated in general terms in international instruments, meets Bentham's criticisms about nonsensical claims of imprescriptability. The importance of rights is demonstrated by their centrality in analyses of proposed laws; their limits are demonstrated by the balancing and judgement that commonly occurs via the formal and informal workings of the parliament.[7]

# 2. A constant conversation

Tim Wilson

Advancing human rights in Australia is best served by keeping debates encroaching on liberty alive amongst the body politic.

So much of the British political tradition around rights is what evolved out of revolution to temper the abuses of feudalist power. For America it was the same, as well as in response to internal opposition to centralised power. What makes Australia unique is that it is a fusion of these traditions that is also absent the protections afforded to Americans and the British to protect their rights. Australia was founded to be a hybrid of the British and American traditions. Australia was founded to be a grand experiment in liberal democratic governance.

Australia may only have been founded from administrative procedure, but it is arguably the most revolutionary of the comparable models of political governance. The expectation is that the greatest bulwark to the abuse of government power is an active citizenry. It is for Australians to stand firm and proud in defence of their universal rights, and failure to do so gives licence to the legislature to encroach on them.

While human rights academics or activists believe that the invocation of these principles amounts to a 'drop mic moment', such rights are actually advanced through the legislative silence of their existence and assumed as the default through the traditions of the common law. They are preserved through persuasion where respect achieves the good for the maximum number of people and dispensable as required to achieve a collective purpose.

In his Tocquevillian analysis, "Political ideology in Australia: The distinctiveness of a Benthamite society",[1] Hugh Collins, a British academic, articulates the uniqueness of Australian political institutions and culture and its approach to the concept of liberty.

In rejecting the overly simplistic conclusion that our Westminster traditions made us an antipodean replica of Westminster, or American federalism made us a Washington clone, he observed:

> Australia's perennial debates and present predicaments may be understood, [and] the differences presented to an American, or British, observer become comprehensible, if one begins by regarding Australia as a Benthamite society.[2]

In defining a Benthamite society, he argued for the importance of utilitarianism to Australia's political culture:

> to reconcile the pursuit of individual interest with the achievement of sovereign interest or greatest happiness . . . This individualism makes [Bentham's] theory anti-collectivist . . . A collectivism that captures utilitarianism's political instruments would always be in conflict with Bentham's commitment to individualism. . . . Although a theory of individual interests, it rejects the notion of natural rights which was central in both the American and the French revolutions. Elie Halévy states Bentham's position succinctly: "Governments were instituted not because man had rights, but because he had none". In an ideology faithful to Bentham's system natural rights will be an alien tradition . . . The rationalist assumptions of Bentham's philosophy signal an approach to politics that is both secular and instrumental . . . there is neither a messianic mission nor return to a classical ideal.[3]

Collins's analysis reflects the practical reality of Australia's tradition of human rights. Our legal inheritance from the common law assumes the rights and freedoms of the individual, while parliament is custodian to decide the public good.

This is not a tradition by accident. The important point to recognise is that this approach did not evolve in a vacuum. As David Kemp, who served in the First, Second, and Third Howard Ministry, argues in his essay, "The Liberals: A short history of Liberalism in Victoria and Australia":

> Liberal ideas that came with the first fleet and its successors had first been formulated by French, English and Scottish thinkers of the Enlightenment, such as John Locke (the social contract), Montesquieu (the balanced constitution), Adam Smith (private-self interest in the market could serve the public good) and David Hume (reason was the way to understand the world and decide on policy).[4]

That does not mean Australia lacks a human rights tradition. Some of our most celebrated national moments reflect individuals asserting themselves against the encroachment of centralized power through utilitarian political traditions, such as:

- The early 1800s Rum Rebellion against the Governor, William Bligh, was fought over the right of free people to contract;
- The 1854 Eureka Stockade was a miners' rebellion against excessive taxation;
- The 1879 first congress of unions was a practical demonstration of the cultural importance of free association in the colonies;
- Full franchise was achieved in 1902 when Australia was the first country in the world to grant women the right to stand for Parliament and vote concurrently;
- In 1967, through a public referendum, Aboriginal and Torres Strait Islander people were respected as full citizens;
- More recently, in 2017, through a mixture of public survey and legislative reform, Australians extended the civil

institution of marriage to same-sex couples.

All occurred without any rigid human rights instruments and were achieved through ongoing public debates around freedom and justice.

Australia's unique approach is a product of the constitutional convention debates of the late nineteenth century that considered the lessons of the French Revolution and the experiment of the American Bill of Rights. Rather than adopt expansive provisions around rights, they limited the Commonwealth's power to legislate on religion,[5] as well as to protect private property.[6] Otherwise, the spirit of Federation overcame Commonwealth powers and these decisions were left to the States.

While Australia played an instrumental role in the negotiation of the Universal Declaration of Human Rights which also laid the groundwork for the later International Covenant on Civil and Political Rights, the parliament has generally been wary of translating them into domestic law. This is because doing so might disrupt pre-existing legal principles.

Part of the parliament's difficulty lies in the fact that modern 'human rights' treaties fail to take seriously the distinction between 'positive' and 'negative' liberty identified by Isaiah Berlin in his famous inaugural lecture at Oxford, *Two Concepts of Liberty*.[7] Berlin recognised that these treaties were negotiated in an atmosphere in which there were tensions that "have led to the great clash of ideologies that dominates our world".[8] He argued that, at the height of the Cold War, these ideologies could be understood in terms of differing attitudes to liberty. He characterized these as positive liberty and negative liberty. An ideology that is committed to negative liberty seeks to answer the question:

> What is the area within which the subject—a person or group of persons—is or should be left to do or be what he is able to do or be, without interference by other persons?[9]

An ideology committed to positive liberty seeks to answer a

different question, namely:

> What, or who, is the source of control or interference that can determine someone to do, or be, this rather than that?[10]

The tension between the two gives rise to different understandings of the purpose of human rights. In liberal democracies, the focus is on protecting individuals against the abuse of government power. In collectivist traditions, the focus is on achieving a sense of community acceptance of state control as a reflection of public policy.

In his history of the International Covenant on Civil and Political Rights, the Austrian human rights lawyer, Manfred Nowak, writes about how Articles 19 and 20, the Articles about freedom of thought and expression, perfectly demonstrate the tension between the socialist and liberal traditions of human rights.

Nowak maintains that according to

> the liberal view, every individual has the freedom to form his or her own opinions free from external indoctrination and to defend them in "the free market of ideas" without fear of repression . . . The zone of legitimate State intervention commences at the point where the expression of an opinion interferes with the rights of others or constitutes an obvious, direct threat to life in society.[11]

He continues:

> According to the socialist view, human rights are, in general, the embodiment of the very essence of the Socialist State and are marked by an "objective conformity of interests between the citizen and the socialist society freed of class antagonism".[12]

It can be distilled down to something simpler. In a liberal democracy, freedom is the default, and the case for interference must be made. In all other political systems, governmental power is default and freedom for the individual must be explicitly permitted. Australia is a liberal democracy.

Positive liberty is really social policy dressed up as 'rights'. Positive liberty cannot be achieved without infringing the rights and freedom of others. For example, any right to health or education is noble in its ambition but compels others to carry the burden of delivery directly. This contradicts the objective of free agency in the liberal tradition. Similarly, while negative liberty is universally anchored and only needs to be constrained to respect the rights and freedom of others, positive liberty is often dependent on the economic progress of a society. Rich societies can deliver higher universal levels of 'the right to health' through affordable access to technologies and treatments, whereas poorer countries cannot meet the same standard. This gives rise to a situation that undermines the concept of universality of human rights.

That positive liberty should not give rise to human rights does not demean its importance. It is part of the perpetual and unending pursuit of justice in society; a pursuit that seeks to provide people with equal opportunity and to redress natural injustices that often occur outside our control.

Human rights within the common law is predicated upon the concept of negative liberty. Thus, within the common law tradition, the case for expanding instruments that compel compliance with human rights is questionable, and occasionally counterproductive. New Zealand's human rights legislation has regularly been used as a legal weapon to trivialize human rights, including limiting the capacity for schools to impose uniform requirements because they violate a student's freedom of expression.[13] In one case, it has even been used by a student to successfully oppose a school imposing neat hairstyling.[14]

The self-expressive rebel in most of us probably has some sympathy. But it is the sort of issue that should be fought at a school council meeting and a contrarian protest at Monday morning assembly. That it was elevated all the way to a national charter of rights does nothing for the social standing of human rights, and can be interpreted as belittling them.

This has partly been the argument by some critics of charters of rights. They are largely designed to prompt consideration of legislation against 'human rights' principles. In practice, these charters can then be weaponized to achieve certain public policy outcomes.

They are not the only instruments that are of dubious benefit in engaging public support for human rights. After consultation, the federal parliament established the Joint Standing Committee on Human Rights. Its establishment was justified on the grounds that it "will enhance the consideration of human rights in Commonwealth legislation" with complementary statements of compatibility to inform legislative development.[15] Theoretically, the committee complements the consideration of legislators in adhering to commitments already undertaken through international treaties. Practically, it subverts democratic public policy makings. As the Julian Leeser rightly argues:

> It is a bureaucracy that has appropriated the name of the Parliament. The Committee is about bureaucrats judging Parliament, rather than the Parliament judging human rights.[16]

While the objectives of academics assessing legislation against international treaties may be superficially noble, it empowers bureaucratic advisers to provide supra-critiques of laws developed by democratic legislators. It does so with scant regard for the justifiability, in a domestic legislative context, of recommendations. In this way, it undermines the socialization often required in balancing rights and freedoms in law.

If Australia truly wants to constrain the freedom of legislators and regulators to impinge on human rights, the best alternative is to develop a bill of rights. A bill of rights enjoys rhetorical support in some quarters. During my term as Australia's Human Rights Commissioner, when the topic was raised with me by members of the public, their support waned quickly when they had to take the principle of the good (e.g. free speech), with the practicality of its application for what were deemed undesirable ends (e.g. repeal of laws like section 18C of the Racial Discrimination Act, which makes it unlawful to offend, insult, humiliate, or intimidate a person on the basis of their race, colour, national or ethnic origin; and possibly even repealing laws requiring plain packaging on tobacco products).

The introduction of a bill of rights probably becomes unworkable following the development of a mature legal system. The development of the legal system of a nation is like a growing garden. At first it is barren and the discussion around the constitution is the parameters of the plot. As legislatures cogitate, the seeds are sewn and legislative flowers bloom. If a bill of rights develops concurrently with a legal system, the law will grow around the guiding stakes it provides. If not, the plants will growly freely based on the cultures present.

The latter is largely Australia's experience. The former is the experience of the United States. But injecting the stakes of a bill of rights after the garden is grown displaces existing law and substitutes rigidity.

It is only through the exploration of debates that we can find a workable approach to the conservation of human rights in a society that seeks to take the whole of the Australian community forward together. As Catherine Renshaw accurately concludes:

> the gravest danger to human rights is constraint on deliberative democracy—limitations on discourse and debate about the conditions under which people can participate in shaping the kind of society in which they live.

Renshaw's conclusions were brought alive during the obscure pathway for Australians to resolve the legal definition of marriage. After thirteen years of debate, the issue eventually ended with a public survey of attitudes to inform the parliament. The survey was legally unnecessary, but assisted those on both sides of the debate by having a concrete evidence-base to reference support for or opposition to the proposal. Critically, it highlighted that the legitimacy of democratic decisions comes not from a victor's satisfaction, but the vanquished accepting loss.

Australians value the principles of human rights, but not in isolation. They sit as part of a broader democratic discussions about rights, responsibilities, and providing a more just society.

This was brought home by the tensions that sat at the heart of the 2009 National Human Rights Consultation led by Father Frank Brennan. In its deliberations about pursuing the appropriate human rights framework, it identified 'hot button' topics that could not be resolved without democratic legitimacy:

> Throughout the Committee's consultations participants kept raising four topics—same-sex marriage, euthanasia, abortion, and religious concerns with the Victorian Charter of Human Rights and Responsibilities—that give rise to intense debate in the community. At the community roundtables, discussion often turned to whether a Human Rights Act would be a help or a hindrance in efforts to improve laws and policies in these areas without polarising the community.[17]

Since these consultations, the necessary instruments to resolve marriage for same-sex couples resulted from a national postal survey to assess the mood of the nation with complex legislation to balance competing rights, while attitudes to abortion and euthanasia remain contested, and an ongoing broader discussion around freedom of religion continues.

Human rights will continue to play a critical part in the national dialogue to inform the development of law and practice in Australia. To make them necessarily relevant requires their adaptation to the constant changing circumstances facing contemporary society.

As Damien Freeman correctly explains, discussions persist absent a rigid legal framework because they are part of a societal dialogue to respect and advance human *interests*. However, that does not mean they are substitutable. Human rights fundamentally identify the principles that frame a discussion. Interests reflect other social and political objectives that need to be considered in the preservation of human rights. And there are many examples—ranging from the trade-off between free speech, privacy and security on digital platforms and health records, property rights and innovation in healthcare and medicine, and the tension between whether we are a post-Christian secular or pluralist society.

Managing these tensions can be informed by academics, activists, or charters, but sustainable preservation within the Australian context requires such tensions to be resolved through democratic debate and decision-making.

# 3. Disagreeing about rights and interests

Emma Dawson

Damien Freeman's essay is an illuminating contribution to the ongoing debate about human rights, and offers useful insights into the operation of our parliamentary democracy at a time when trust in political leaders and institutions is under significant pressure. Whether it offers a prescription for "rescuing human rights in Australia", however, is disputable.

Freeman opens persuasively by quoting Philip Larkin, whose poetry, Freeman says, "gives expression to the tone of post-war Britain in all its weary and mundane smallness". That Freeman enlists Larkin's voice to open his argument is curiously apposite, given the analysis of human rights discourse that follows. Long regarded as a chronicler of small-minded, middle-class lives steeped in racism and misogyny, Larkin is being reassessed by a new generation of critics as a subversively progressive artist whose poetry subtly interrogates conventional attitudes to class, gender, and authority.

This ideological tension, between the forces of traditionalism and progress, besets Freeman's argument that human rights are lost "in the long grass". The result is a sophisticated argument concerning the difference between human rights and human *interests,* one which is solidly grounded in political theory and moral philosophy, but which ultimately fails to persuade the reader of the merits of the argument against Australia's institutional approach to human rights that Freeman has chosen to defend: that of federal parliamentarian Julian Leeser.

The essay rests on the fundamental question of whether human rights are intrinsic, or assigned by humans to one another. Arguing convincingly for the latter answer, Freeman draws on Richard Rorty's position that it is sentiment rather than rationality that drives us to assign rights to other humans, essentially through the creation of empathy built through shared interests.

Freeman then draws on the work of renowned political philosopher Raymond Geuss, who has long argued that human rights are not intrinsic, or natural, but rather *positive*[1]—that is, they "depend on specific positive political decisions"—to advance his argument. Citing an interview Geuss gave to Lawrence Hamilton in 2013,[2] Freeman makes a strong case that rights, where they have been agreed upon through political processes, are, to use Geuss's word, 'trumps', in that the invocation of them stops further debate or discussion.

The essay then proceeds by reference to Geuss's well established argument that many of the things people assert as human rights are, in fact, human *interests*, and that by declaring their individual interests to be rights, people effectively shut down debate and thwart the political process of finding ways to live together in their differences.

Freeman argues persuasively that the misrepresentation of human interests as human rights is damaging our democratic processes and institutions. Indeed, the early part of the essay can be read as a strong rebuke to the proponents of 'identity politics', in which individual interests based on differentiating factors of a person's identity (race, gender, sexuality, religion, for example) are often asserted as universal human rights.

Freeman makes clear that the use of human rights as 'trumps' in arguments about the intersectional aspects of political and social discrimination serves to shut down the essential civic conversation through which we negotiate a way to live harmoniously in a globalised, multicultural world. That is, his early argument can be read as a cry for us to step back from demanding our individual interests be treated as inalienable rights, so as to engage better in the political process of identifying the things we have in common and compromising to reach agreement on the best possible way forward for the society we share.

There is merit to the argument that some people's increasingly loud insistence that their interests are rights is preventing our democratic system from working, and that this is contributing to the growing disillusionment with democratic institutions and widespread disengagement from our system of government.

The first half of Freeman's essay is a more sophisticated and persuasive argument against the more egregious indulgences of identity politics and its contribution to the fragmentation of society than one usually encounters in the political debate. As such it is a welcome contribution to the discourse.

The later part of the essay, though, struggles to persuade; perhaps because, as the author himself notes, he is apparently attempting to justify a conservative opposition to human rights for political minorities through the framework of a Marxist critique.

The second half of the essay is concerned with defending the position of Liberal Party MP Julian Leeser on the operation of the Australian Human Rights Commission and the Australian Parliament's Joint Committee on Human Rights. As Freeman notes, Leeser believes that "the first needs to be reformed and the second abolished".

The fundamental problem in this part of the essay is that, having skilfully demonstrated the problem with accepting as universal human rights things that are merely individual human interests, the author is unable to define which things fall into each category.

Further, the language in this section of the essay is less distinct and Freeman abandons the early rigour with which he defines terminology: for example, he uncritically accepts Leeser's reference to "the pub test" as something by which society should assess the validity of an asserted right; this is a nebulous concept, and its inclusion as equivalent to the deliberate language of political theory on which Freeman's earlier arguments rest is incongruous and frustrating.

Leeser's position on rights versus interests is inconsistent and certainly ideological. For example, he apparently supports property rights as rights rather than interests, but takes issue with several other rights included in international treaties to which the work of the Joint Committee on Human Rights must have regard—such as "the right to holiday pay, paid maternity leave; free education; the right to social security; and the right to an 'adequate standard of living'."

Freeman quotes from Leeser's 2018 B'nai B'rith Human Rights Address, "Human Rights Hijacked", in which he asks rhetorically, "These things might be nice to have but really would most Australians consider them to be human rights? And more so than the right to property and freedom of contract?"

While Leeser has been a strong defender of Section 18C of the Racial Discrimination Act 1975 against repeated assaults from many of his coalition colleagues, he evinces in his address an ideological opposition to other rights advocated by what he calls "left wing and social justice groups".

It is these groups, Leeser declares, that have 'hijacked' the infrastructure of human rights institutions in Australia. Leeser asserts that the reports of the Joint Committee on Human Rights, on which he serves, are often "merely a collateral attack on the government's legislative agenda in the form of rehashed talking points from [these groups] that have no connection to 'real' human rights".

Herein lies the problem with Leeser's critique, and Freeman's defence of it: neither man explains what he believes to be 'real' human rights. Beyond freedom from acts of genocide, it is unclear whether Freeman or Leeser recognise any other established rights at all pertaining to humanity or to groups within certain socio-political communities.

While Leeser's criticism of the operation of the parliamentary committee is presented as an objection to its 'bureaucratic' nature, it in fact seems to stem from his discomfort with the rights the committee is bound to consider: he bemoans the absence of property rights, and ridicules the right to an "adequate standard of living".

Of course, the defence of property rights is an inherently capitalist position, while the defence of the right to an adequate standard of living is a socialist one.

It is hard to escape the conclusion that Leeser's complaints, and Freeman's defence of them, spring from their mistaken conviction that the rights set out in the treaties and statutes that govern the work of the commission and the committee are not genuine rights at all.

In fact, to use Geuss's language, it would appear that Leeser believes his interests are being trumped by illegitimate rights. His crusade is not actually to reform the processes of institutions, but to re-prosecute the case that certain rights recognised in the framework within which Australia's human rights institutions operate ought be reclassified as merely interests.

As Freeman makes clear in the first part of the essay, conversations about human interests are critical to the political process, but, surely, at some point, we need to accept the collective decision arrived at through that process.

In the second half of the twentieth century, following the atrocities of World War II, developed nations were able to agree that certain interests constituted human rights. Since then, other rights have emerged, often through the collective political action of minorities, and have come to be recognised as rights within international treaties.

Progress—the evolution of the human condition—demands that power be disrupted and distributed more equally, and this necessitates the recognition of new rights for different groups from time to time. That some traditionalists find the collective decision to award rights to new communities of interest objectionable is not grounds to overturn the collective decision or to abolish the structures that underpin the administration of human rights in our parliaments or civic institutions. Rather, it is an ideological battle that should be waged as part of that political process that determines the status of human interests in the collective good.

Indeed, if we dismantle the architecture of human rights because of an ideological objection to majority decisions, then the framework that guides those essential conversations about how to balance our competing interests—which Leeser acknowledges occurs in other parliamentary committees, and Freeman makes clear is indispensable to the political process—will collapse.

In an otherwise thoughtful and persuasive essay, Freeman fails to interrogate the clearly ideological basis of Leeser's criticism of the Australian Human Rights Commission and the Joint Committee on Human Rights, or to investigate the core question of who decides what are human rights and what merely human interests. These omissions fundamentally weaken his otherwise excellent argument about the need to differentiate between rights and interests, and to ensure that we continue the difficult but essential task of collectively balancing our competing interests to forge and protect a harmonious, pluralistic democracy.

That this imperative is the basis for the perpetuation of our human rights discourse is ably demonstrated in Catherine Renshaw's essay. Renshaw illuminates competing theories of human rights, outlining the dominant metaphysical arguments in Western thought and concisely examining the validations of human rights in other cultures. She identifies those rights that are widely accepted as *universal*, and notes that:

> For most who have written in this vein, the list of core, inter-culturally valid rights are the same as the non-derogable rights listed in the International Covenant on Civil and Political Rights: the right to life;

freedom from torture, slavery, arbitrary arrest and imprisonment; recognition before the law; and freedom of thought, conscience and religion.

Renshaw mounts a strong critique of the universalist approach, and provides a compelling argument for the political conception of human rights, in which the practice of human rights in modern societies "is the process by which political institutions and communities are challenged and then forced to either justify suppression and exclusion or to become more inclusive and egalitarian".

This framework convincingly challenges Leeser's objection to the expansion of human rights to include new rights for people based on communities of identity. As Renshaw makes clear, under the political conception, the inventory of human rights is not closed; rather, it is "subject to revision or extension".

Her masterful essay is, in effect, a compelling rebuttal of Leeser's arguments against the expansion of human rights and the operation of the Australian Human Rights Commission and the Joint Committee on Human Rights; for, if human rights are useful at all, it is as the underpinning of our political system of negotiating the good society.

Ultimately, as Renshaw demonstrates, "the gravest danger to human rights is constraint on deliberative democracy—limitations on discourse and debate about the conditions under which people can participate in shaping the kind of society in which they live".

If, as Renshaw argues so persuasively, "Upholding and reinforcing the ideal of deliberative democracy . . . is the ultimate answer to the question of how to rescue human rights", then the refusal, inherent in Lesser's argument, to accommodate a contested discourse and the development and expansion of our understanding of human rights is not a defence of human rights at all, but an attack on their very foundations.

# 4. Our common lives

Nicholas Aroney

Damien Freeman poses an important question: should deliberation about the ends and means of our common life be framed in terms of human rights or human interests? Human interests are about the substantial things that human beings need and desire, such as life and health, peace and prosperity, friendship and community, meaning and purpose, love and understanding. We pursue ends like these when we engage in conversations about the ordering of our lives together. Human rights, on the other hand, are trumps. They are the grounds on which such conversations about the common good are stopped before they can even begin.

Human interests are, therefore, the proper substance of our deliberations together as a community. However, Freeman does not want us to dispense with rights altogether. This is because human rights name those matters of human interest that should not be up for debate. We should never deliberate about whether massacring innocent civilians might somehow be justifiable. We should never consider the use of instruments of coercion to compel people to adopt ideologically correct opinions or abandon their religious beliefs. There are lines in politics that should never be crossed.

But if rights are to function properly in our society they need to be kept in their place. They are no substitute for conversations about how best to secure the many good things that humans need and rightly desire. Rights should not be allowed to expand and colonise our communities so completely that our conversations are always and only couched in the language of entitlements. To do so is to enact a distorted vision of humanity and the common good.

Freeman's point is well-made. However, there is a background assumption in the argument that also needs to be considered. Although his essay begins with 'our life in common', this is soon transposed into 'the political'. It seems that these ongoing conversations about our lives in common have to do with the domain of government. But politics is not simply about those matters that concern us all as a community of human beings. It is also the realm of the coercive. While it sounds benign to imagine us participating in so many sweet conversations about the shape of our lives together, when these discussions are political, we are talking about the exercise of the policing powers of the state. And that is one reason why rights are so important, for they protect us from the exercise by the state of the instruments of physical coercion which it claims as its exclusive prerogatives.

Emphasising the coercive nature of the state might be thought to turn the argument back in the direction of rights. To an extent that is true. But it is not the whole picture. This is because there is another assumption in Freeman's argument that warrants exploration. On Freeman's account, our deliberations occur in a space defined in the simple, all-encompassing terms of 'our common life'. However, our daily lives are many times more complex than this. We are born into families. We grow up in neighbourhoods. We attend local schools. We join nearby sporting clubs and socialise in coffee shops, bars and pubs. We gather locally for worship and volunteer for charitable organisations. We are employed by commercial enterprises and engage in joint endeavours of many kinds. And in all of these contexts we are engaged in conversations about the ordering of lives together. Only a fractional aspect of our participation in these undertakings concerns matters that are civic or political in the sense that they involve the coercive powers of the state. And even the political is for us divided into its local, state, and federal dimensions.

Rights are important in demarcating the boundaries of these spheres of human life. Without rights of free association, all would be in danger of collapsing into an undifferentiated whole. Families, neighbourhoods, schools, clubs, enterprises, religions, and charities contribute to the securing of human welfare in manifold ways. But their capacity to secure these goods depends on their powers of self-organisation and independence. As a consequence, Freeman's distinction between human interests and human rights applies to every one of these spheres. The manifold associations and institutions that constitute our society depend on their ability to pursue those things that make our lives worthwhile. But if they are to pursue these ends effectively, they cannot be reduced to mere satellites of the state. Legally enforceable rights guarantee their independence from external interference so they can be free to pursue those goods that governments cannot provide or guarantee. Within each of these spheres—Edmund Burke's 'little platoons'—there are conversations about how best to secure the manifold goods of human life. However, these internal conversations will be distorted if conducted in the vocabulary of rights.

Rights language is especially corrosive when individualised conceptions of entitlement intrude into those associations and institutions where vital human interests are best secured when we lay aside our personal preferences and act for the benefit of others. To be married, or to be a parent, is to lay down my rights and live for the good of my spouse and my children. To be a good student, or a good teacher, is to commit myself to the disciplines of teaching and learning. I cannot be an effective team-mate, employee, or volunteer if I constantly demand my rights and entitlements. There are goods in human life that can only be secured through disciplines of austerity, abstinence and self-denial. Personal qualities such as prudence, courage, temperance and justice, alongside faith, hope and love, are the cardinal and spiritual virtues on which so many good things depend. The individualised rights language that too often dominates our politics is destructive of these goods, particularly when it colonises the spheres of human life which depend on the cultivation of personal qualities such as self-restraint and self-discipline.

In her defence of human rights, Catherine Renshaw expresses concern that societies which place emphasis on duties and responsibilities are liable to become authoritarian and hierarchical. She cites Yash Ghai to the effect that such talk betokens social, economic, or political subordination and the perpetuation of inequalities. But rights talk can lead to similar outcomes; it just depends on whose rights get enforced, and at whose expense. Liberalism always comes with its hard edges. It finds it difficult to tolerate those it regards as intolerant, and it is willing to exclude people in the name of inclusion, as Israel Folau has discovered. Rights talk can never mean that everyone's rights prevail all of the time. Someone's rights have to give way, and when they do, there can be very unpleasant practical consequences, like the loss of a job and the destruction of one's career.

All of this gives us reason to doubt the wisdom of enacting statutory charters of rights of the kind that have been adopted in Victoria, the Australian Capital Territory, and now Queensland. The purpose of the charters is not to entrench a set of rights which the courts enforce as conversation-ending trumps, but rather to engage the courts in a political dialogue with governments and legislatures in the shared tasks of governance. Under the charters, ministers and members of parliament are required to issue statements of compatibility with human rights when introducing proposed laws. Parliamentary committees are required to prepare reports which assess whether proposed laws are compatible with human rights. Civil servants, government departments, and public agencies are required under the charters to administer the law in a manner that is compatible with human rights. And finally, the courts are required to interpret statutes in a manner that, so far as possible, is compatible with human rights or else to make declarations of the incompatibility of such laws with human rights.

Under the charters, every branch of government is subjected to a regime of compulsory human rights talk. This does not mean that human rights operate as trumps which, through the intervention of the courts, bring political conversations to an end. Rather, political discourse is subjected to a thorough-going juridification. Consideration of substantial human interests may still guide and shape political decisions, but all such determinations are ultimately subjected to juridical assessment in terms of their effect on human rights. Human rights are not so much trumps as they are the rules according to which the game must ultimately be played.

This has knock-on effects for our families, our associations, our religions, and our communities. For in this juridification of politics there is an individualisation of rights. Juridification is meant to provide a bulwark against state power, but the charters only protect the rights of individual persons. This places collective organisations and institutions in a double bind: the rights guaranteed by the charters encourage individuals to demand that organisations change their practices to accommodate their personal preferences, while the juridification of politics weakens the capacity of organisations to appeal to the human interests of their membership to resist such demands. The Victorian Charter may use the word 'responsibilities' in its title as Renshaw points out, but the only responsibilities recognised in its operative provisions are to respect the rights of others, whatever that may mean in practice.

The rights of individuals are also reduced in the charters to discrete lists. This is necessarily the case when abstract entitlements of right are enacted into law. But the lists are also selective, and revealingly so. Not all the rights set out the International Covenant on Civil and Political Rights, let alone the International Covenant on

Social and Economic Rights, find their way into the human rights charters. Under Article 18 of the International Covenant on Civil and Political Rights, for example, state parties are required to respect the liberty of parents to ensure the religious and moral education of their children in accordance with their religious convictions. But this right is strangely missing from Australia's human rights charters. It receives only very attenuated recognition in the Australian Capital Territory's charter, and none at all in Victoria and Queensland.

Under the charters, human rights are made the currency of the realm. But because they are expressed in such abstract and general terms, the rights contained in the charters must be limited, for otherwise there will be contradictions between them. As Mary Ann Glendon has pointed out in her book, *Rights Talk*, when we assert rights in absolute terms, "we are expressing infinite and impossible desires—to be completely free, to possess things totally, to be captains of our fate, and masters of our souls". Thus, the Victorian Charter says that while every person has the "right to freedom of expression", this may be subject to lawful restrictions reasonably necessary to respect the rights and reputation of other persons. This must necessarily be the case. But if this is so, why call them 'rights'? Such language encourages a climate of public discourse in which there are clashes between competing rights fuelled by underlying fundamental disagreements about their nature, content, and scope. It is not clear that the result has been especially edifying. In this context rights talk tends to become either a fuel that inflames our differences or a pastiche that obscures them. It is hardly a formula to resolve them.

# 5. Splitting our differences

Jennifer Cook

Modern-day 'rights talk' in Australia can have a chilling effect on debate. As Damien Freeman suggests, once someone asserts what they call a 'right' and another asserts a second (usually competing) 'right', it is often the case that conversation simply ceases. Rights can therefore operate like trumps, particularly when the assertion of an issue (characterised as a 'right') is framed in terms of an entitlement or an absolute right.

In many cases, 'rights' have become a matter of individuals doing whatever they want in the name of happiness or their own personal freedom. According to Mary Ann Glendon, a law professor at Harvard University, "rights in the current American dialect are the expression of desires the drafters of the Bill of Rights viewed with suspicion—to be completely free, to possess things totally, to be treated justly without being asked to act justly."[1] Glendon uses the controversial American example of flag burning where someone says, "The way I see it, I buy a flag. It's my property. So I have a right to do anything I want with it,"[2] which is stated in such absolute terms that any response (other than the diametrically opposed, "no you can't") is difficult. Rights can operate as trumps in Australia too, as evidenced by the issue of same-sex marriage. Proponents and opponents were generally so polarised in their 'rights talk' (relying on rights against discrimination or equality versus the right to religious freedom) that dialogue became practically impossible. Compromise under these circumstances is elusive.

But does the assertion of a 'right' really have to be the end of the conversation? The very characterisation of rights as trumps is unhelpful as this can also end a conversation about rights.[3] Freeman's characterisation of rights as trumps implies that there is no ability to compromise (with the implication being, why bother trying?) and misunderstands that it is completely uncontroversial that rights and rights claims come into conflict. Even in court cases, the assertion or claim of a right does not usually operate as a trump or necessarily lead to a quick decision. The assertion of a right is actually just the beginning of what is often needed, namely to do significant further work, engage in discussion, and make substantive submissions.[4]

Admittedly, the issue of human rights is a complex one, with a multiplicity of differing theories of human rights and differing views as to what constitutes a 'right'. The real problem with rights, however, is not that one right conflicts with, or 'trumps', another right, or that there are differing views about rights. The answer does not lie in accepting that conversation ceases once a right is claimed. It is not an answer, as Freeman suggests, to relegate rights to the domain of the judiciary but otherwise not engage in rights talk in politics or in the public square. Indeed, according to academics Louise Chappell, John Chesterman, and Lisa Hill, "the articulation and protection of human rights are not only legal processes but also intensely political ones".[5] That may be, but Glendon decries what she calls the "impoverishment of our political discourse".[6] In the Twitter era and rapid pace of the twenty-first century, with discourse reduced to catchphrases, improved rights discourse will be difficult.[7] Difficult though it may be, human rights in Australia will not be rescued until, at least, the problem of how rights talk occurs is addressed, and the quality of debate by politicians and across society is improved and extended.

Those merely asserting a right often expect that this will trump competing claims and resolve the issue. However, the conversation does not need to, and should not, stop before it has even begun. There needs to be more than just superficial conversation in catchphrases or in emotive language—there needs to be sensible, intelligent, and reasoned debate and an understanding of the public justification for the right that is being asserted.[8] This involves considering at the outset whether what is being asserted is actually a right or, instead, is better characterised as something like an issue of concern or a mere preference or a matter of social justice. If the issue is best characterised as a right, consideration then needs to turn to the substance of the right and how this might be balanced with other rights.[9] In the view of the New Zealand professor of law and philosophy, Jeremy Waldron, where there is a contested human rights claim, there is a need to "work one's way back" to the foundations of the right claimed.[10] He says:

> The predicaments and difficulties of social life are multiplying at an alarming rate (think of some of the puzzles posed by the new reproductive technology). An articulated structure of values—that is a sense of what is deep and what is superficial among our evaluations, how they are connected and which of them rests on what assumptions of fact—helps us to order the moral resources we have at our disposal to deal with challenges.[11]

Thus, there is a need to drill down into what underpins an asserted right and, in doing so, seek compromise. Discussion must be widespread, requiring engagement by politicians and involvement of citizens, including the involvement of those traditionally underrepresented and "bringing ... more new players on the political scene."[12] In Glendon's view, it is the very act of discussing differences that will lessen intolerance and division and, in this process, common ground will be found:

> It is becoming plain that our liberal regime of equality and personal freedom depends, more than most theorists of liberalism have been willing to admit, on the existence and support of certain social assumptions and practices: the belief that each and every human

being possesses great and inherent value, the willingness to respect the rights of others even at the cost of some disadvantages to one's self; the ability to defer some immediate benefits for the sake of long-range goals and a regard for reason-giving and civility in public discourse.[13]

It is not just absolutist rights talk that is a problem. The proliferation of what are characterised as 'rights' also impedes discourse and makes it more complicated. The number of claimed rights is expanding at a rapid pace, making conflict inevitable and finding solutions and compromise difficult, if not impossible.[14] This rights inflation has occurred, in part, due to the increasing number of rights recognised in United Nations treaties and in international instruments. In 2013, a Danish research group, the Freedom Rights Project, counted the number of individual rights provisions in United Nations and European human rights instruments and found that they totalled 667 in the United Nations system and 710 in the Council of Europe![15]

Proliferation of 'rights' has also occurred as a result of an increasing tendency to assign the label 'right' to a vast array of matters, some of which would, perhaps, be considered more appropriately as a matter of social or economic policy. This encourages disputes rather than discussion and can mean underlying problems are not addressed. According to one legal scholar, Cass Sunstein:

> A claimed right to clean air or water or to safe products and workplaces makes little sense in light of the need for close assessment in particular cases of the advantages of greater environmental protection or more safety, as compared with the possibly accompanying disadvantages—higher prices, lower wages, less employment, more poverty.[16]

There is clearly a need to reframe the debate. Freeman helpfully suggests that instead of 'rights talk', discourse should instead principally focus on human interests. Freeman refers to Michael Casey's suggestion that matters of human flourishing should be discussed in the context of promoting the human interests contributing to flourishing. In a similar vein, the Canadian professor of sociology, Dominique Clément, suggests that concerns or complaints be framed in terms of social justice. Like Casey's suggestion to focus on matters of interests as contributing to human flourishing, Clément considers such a reframing of dialogue would facilitate the pursuit by individuals of what, in their view, constitutes a good life.[17]

Some suggest that the 'rights' that are the subject of discourse should be pared down to fundamental rights (for instance, the civil and political rights enumerated in the *International Covenant on Civil and Political Rights*), with a view to stopping the creation or elaboration of new rights. The Freedom Rights Project takes this view. It has called for a halt to rights inflation and suggests that human rights bodies focus on the enforcement of existing core rights rather than creating new rights.[18] Dialogue about social and economic rights should then be cast in broader social terms, as Clément suggests, or there is a risk that courts or rights commissions will end up determining matters such as the amount of welfare payments. According to Clément, "if social justice is a dialogue around grievances against the state and society, then human rights are those core principles that make the dialogue possible."[19] Clément uses poverty as an example of a matter that should not be the subject of 'rights talk':

> Human rights is a poor language for addressing complex issues such as poverty. Poverty as social justice is not just about lack of money but limits on the capability of individuals; education and health care are important because they improve a person's quality of life and ability to earn an income and be free of poverty. The solution, therefore, is more systemic than a right to employment. The implications of unemployment are more profound than a lack of income—it affects self-worth, confidence and capability.[20]

Glendon says it is not straightforward "how the public forum . . . could be reclaimed for genuine and transparent political discourse."[21] There is pervasive disinterest in, even contempt for, politics, but this makes the need for improved dialogue even more urgent. Not only do politicians need to engage in genuine and transparent political discourse among themselves, but, importantly, they need to engage with, and to hear, the concerns and viewpoints of a variety of citizens and stakeholders. According to Renshaw:

> Decisions that affect people's lives ... must be transparent, fair, broad, participatory, inclusive, and wide-ranging, and the marginalised and vulnerable, who are after all the primary intended beneficiaries of human rights must be able to participate.

It is, as Renshaw asserts, constraints on deliberative democracy that threaten human rights.

In recent times, there has been a failure of discourse at the highest levels in Australia, with some politicians variously expressing contempt for international law, exhibiting a lack of political will to engage in rights debate, or simply ignoring human rights issues altogether. There is, at times, an arrogant, nationalistic attitude of some that it is up to Australians to determine what constitutes human rights and the substance of Australia's obligations under international treaties. In a 2014 opinion piece, Ben Saul, a professor of law at the University of Sydney, deplored the human rights talk by Australian government officials, describing an attitude of hubris when it comes to international obligations that are the subject of treaties ratified by Australia (but often not implemented into domestic law). He gave the example of a minister for immigration who "spat the dummy on international law," with that particular Minister saying "'this parliament should decide what our obligations are under these conventions—not those who seek to direct us otherwise from places outside this country'".[22]

The Australian government took a similar stance ten years earlier in response to the United Nations Human Rights Committee's finding that Australia had infringed the rights of Tasmanian Nicholas Toonen. In the years since the Toonen decision, following criticism of Australia's human rights record (in relation to matters such as indigenous rights), the government denounced the United Nations committee system established to monitor treaty compliance, calling for it to be 'overhauled'.[23] Prime Minister John Howard "affirmed the 'determination [of] this government to ensure that matters affecting Australia are resolved by Australians within Australia.'"[24] In more recent times, there has often been a similar dismissive attitude to disapproval voiced by United Nations institutions relating to, for instance, the treatment of asylum seekers arriving by boat. This dismissive attitude extends not only to international organisations but also to engagement with Australian organisations or individual advocates who do not share the government's views. There have been instances where non-governmental organisations, with opposing perspectives on asylum seekers and other rights issues, have had difficulty gaining official access and being heard by members of parliament and other decision makers.[25]

This failure of leadership by Australian parliamentarians on rights issues is characterised by a broader disinclination to engage in discussion of important issues. According to Australian National University professor and former Liberal opposition leader, John Hewson, commenting on the government's campaigning leading up to the 18 May 2019 election day:

> Not only is it detrimental to good government and the national interest that politics has become an opportunistic, short-term game of point scoring and blame shifting, indulgent and mostly negative, but our political masters now seem to have lost their moral compass . . . Their endgame is simply winning at all costs, even at the expense of decency, compassion and principle . . . Rather than present and debate substantive policy, the focus is increasingly on delivering the clever sound bite, or slogan, or performing some mostly silly, exaggerated, stunt. Key issues and challenges are mostly kicked down the road, rather than addressed or solved, sometimes left for the next generation to deal with.[26]

Not only are members of parliament (particularly those forming the executive) often dismissive of international rights institutions and Australian rights organisations, human rights implications are often ignored or dismissed in the process of domestic lawmaking, frequently justified on national security or exigency grounds. For example, anti-terrorism legislation introduced in 2005 was dealt with on an exigent basis, passing through both Houses rapidly without time for meaningful consultation on potential adverse human rights implications.[27] This scenario was repeated recently when, following the attacks on two Christchurch mosques in March 2019, stringent new powers relating to social media and web hosting services became law after being announced on a Tuesday (2 April 2019) and passed on a Thursday (4 April 2019), with less than an hour of debate in parliament.[28] Both parties have promised a review of this legislation by a committee after the May 2019 election. No one doubts that issues arose from the Christchurch attacks that may have required steps to be taken by Australian legislators. However, that passing laws now and considering the impact later is detrimental to the rights of Australians is recognised to be problematic: for instance, the *Australian Financial Review* reported that "Law Council president Arthur Moses SC said despite best intentions laws formulated as a knee-jerk reaction to a tragic event did not necessarily mean good legislation and may have tragic consequences".[29] This problem of lack of meaningful consideration of rights implications in lawmaking needs to be addressed by broadened discourse and, as American political theorist Patrick Deneen suggests, a renewed, and perhaps increased, focus on civil participation and more engagement at the local level.[30]

In addition to broadening discourse and encouraging greater engagement on rights issues, there is also the need in Australia to address the underlying human rights framework itself. Given that Australia lacks a constitutional or statutory bill of rights and empowers parliament to enact laws to implement international law into domestic law, it is the principal role of the parliament in Australia's human rights framework to give direction to the judiciary through its legislation (for instance, anti-discrimination legislation). It is this predominance of parliament that has served majority interests but not necessarily the interests of minority groups, particularly Indigenous Australians.[31] Chappell, Chesterman, and Hill point out that "for some, uncritical faith in the judgment of elected representatives to protect rights is badly misplaced."[32] They are critical of the majoritarian system in terms of its ability to enforce rights, which "'places rights of vulnerable minority groups at the mercy of the will of the majority.'"[33]

An opinion piece in the *Sydney Morning Herald*, headlined "Why Politicians Only Pretend to Care about Low Income Earners", explored this notion that the Australian majoritarian system makes it practically impossible to address minority issues. In commenting on why neither of the major parties would increase payments to unemployed workers, Ross Gittens refers to the rationale put forward by Labor's shadow minister for social services, Linda Burney: "it's because too many voters—including Labor voters no doubt—would disapprove."[34] According to one Australian international law scholar, Hilary Charlesworth, "in this sense, political majorities often tacitly connive in the oppression of minorities".[35] Another human rights lawyer, Frank Brennan, agrees that "the members of entrenched and unpopular minorities often find little consolation at the ballot box".[36] The Australian Catholic Bishops echo this difficulty of addressing minority interests in their statement for the 2019 federal election, in which they implore politicians to focus on the poor and vulnerable, particularly Indigenous Australians and asylum-seekers.[37]

The challenges arising from the supremacy of the parliament in the Australian political system are complicated by the fact that, according to professor of constitutional law at the University of Melbourne, Cheryl Saunders, "the stated protection offered by the Australian constitution is too arbitrary and patchy. The scope of rights protection is unclear and its rationale complex".[38] While the High Court has played an important role and has sought to address human rights issues over the years, controversially recognising an implied freedom of political communication,[39] and more recently in the High Court's increasing engagement with international law, "judges' hands are tied when parliament is explicit in its intention to limit rights".[40]

It is perhaps overly optimistic to expect that voters will be aware enough, or care enough, to vote against governments that fail to enforce human rights or prioritise minority rights or interests. This would mean prioritising rights issues over matters having a more personal impact, such as proposed tax cuts or the superannuation reform agendas of parties. Against this background, Chappell, Chesterman, and Hill argue that politicians in this country must "consider what steps they will take towards adopting a contemporary view of rights and the subsequent new arrangements for their protection."[41] While opinions differ, they argue that a statutory bill of rights, rather than a bill of rights enshrined in the Constitution, would enable the legislature to continue its dominant human rights role but would provide a greater framework for the legislature in its role of legislating in relation to rights, and a better guide for the judiciary in its role of adjudicating rights.[42] A statutory bills of rights would:

> have the capacity to reinvigorate a rights culture within parliament as it forces legislators to assess all bills at the time of drafting and enactment for their rights implications. It asks politicians to wear rights-tinted glasses when undertaking legislative duties. Rights are injected into the work of parliament.[43]

It is beyond the scope of this essay to consider the merits of a statutory bill of rights and explore arguments of those opposing this step. However, in recasting dialogue about human rights in Australia, the issue of whether there should be a constitutional or statutory bill or charter of rights merits further examination.

In a new, more patient, and substantive debate on rights, other steps should also be considered, including reinforcing or expanding the role of existing rights committees of parliament, or even giving consideration to the establishment of new rights bodies outside of the parliament, such as a quasi-judicial rights council like France's Conseil Constitutionnel, that would examine, and provide an opinion (albeit non-binding) on whether bills are compatible with domestic human rights legislation and international rights instruments.[44] Freeman is incorrect in suggesting that rights institutions are part of the problem. Rights institutions should be strengthened, not diluted, and play a key role. Renshaw agrees: "institutions such as the Australian Human Rights Commission have a critical role to play in fostering debate and creating conditions for consensus in circumstances of reasonable disagreement".

What is critical at this point is not being precipitous—arriving at or defining the solution (or discounting a possible solution) to the problem with 'rights talk' in Australia—but acknowledging that rights need to be rescued in Australia by engendering a genuine intellectual discussion about human rights across all sections of Australian society. This means, as Renshaw says, that all opinions are relevant—those of religious leaders, philosophers, lawyers, academics, politicians, and, indeed the opinions of Australians who may not be rights experts but relevantly bring to the debate their life experience including being able to inform lawmakers how laws impact on them and on their communities. Non-governmental organisations, rights bodies, and the media also have their own unique (although in some cases, complementary) roles to play in rights discourse. The discussions should start with the basics, and progress from there. A law lecturer at the University of South Australia, Sarah Moulds, suggests that, in South Australia at least, "it is time to start a real conversation with the community about what rights protection looks like."[45] Discussion should then move to considering possible changes to the human rights framework in Australia, including the possibility of parliament enacting a statutory bill of rights or establishing new rights bodies.

Human rights will not be rescued in Australia without a change of rights culture, both within government institutions and across society, involving the recasting of debate and political discourse.[46] Proper debate cannot occur in a polarised, absolutist, and heated way, or be conducted on an exclusive basis by the political elite. Human rights in Australia can be rescued if there is a commitment by politicians and society as a whole to tolerant, respectful, transparent, and inclusive debate with a view to reaching agreement on rights and the rights framework in this country. At the end of the day, it may just be possible to "'split at least some of our differences.'"[47]

# 6. Human rights versus citizenship

Bryan S. Turner

This response from a sociologist to the two essays by Damien Freeman and Catherine Renshaw could, in principle, be very brief: there is no sociology of human rights.[1] Generally speaking, sociologists have either ignored the global growth of human rights or expressed deep scepticism regarding their generality, practicality, and effective enforcement. On these grounds, it is easy for me to concur with the doubts, anxieties, and criticisms raised so effectively by Freeman and Renshaw. However, the problem I wish to address in this response concerns the relationship between citizen rights and human rights. Many of the rights discussed by Freeman, especially in his comments on Leeser—such as the right to a paid holiday, paid maternity leave, free education, the right to social security, and the right to an adequate standard of living—do not look like human rights, but they are certainly recognisable as the social rights of citizens if we are, for example, thinking of typical European welfare states.

This distinction between human and social rights is not trivial, because, as I will explore in this rejoinder, citizenship presupposes the existence of sovereign states with the capacity to enforce duties and recognise rights. One obvious difference between human and social rights is that there is no universal declaration of duties despite attempts to create one in the Valencia Declaration of Human Duties and Responsibilities (1998). By contrast, citizenship rights typically depend on corresponding duties, and hence we can think of citizenship entitlements in terms of 'contributory rights'. For example, when I pay my taxes, I have the expectation of a right to receive healthcare and other benefits in my old age.[2] I acknowledge, however, that, while the idea of correlativity of rights and duties is recognised in legal theory, there are many cases were this relationship does not hold.[3]

One other issue is that the enforcement of human rights is limited by, for example, the extent of international agreements. So, for example, the courts in the United States have generally resisted the intrusion of human rights legislation into their legal proceedings. For instance, the International Covenant on Civil and Political Rights is not incorporated into domestic law in the United States. Thus, in the case of Guantanamo, human rights organizations could criticise the actions of the Bush Administration, but they were forced to fight the cases concerning torture in court with American law. In more general terms, American courts have resisted the growth of legal pluralism from other legal traditions especially in recent years from the Shari'a.

Sovereign states, as the political and legal framework of national citizenship, have ample means to create rights and duties, and to enforce or expunge them. States can create or redesign institutions in the name of rights. Renshaw gives two examples. In the 2017 Marriage Amendment (Definition and Religious Freedoms) Act, the state effectively redefined marriage. In Renshaw's other example, the action of Rosa Parks in asserting her rights on public transport where the principle of segregated buses was challenged in *Browder v Gayle* and confirmed by the Supreme Court under the Equal Protection Clause of the Fourteenth Amendment. Was this event an example of the 'practice' of human rights or is it what, as a sociologist, Engin Isin would define as 'an act of citizenship'?[4] American historians generally regard this event as a catalyst in the progress of civil—not human—rights.

Do these terminological differences—human, social, civil rights—

matter? They can in fact tell us a great deal about the historical and social location of rights—and the consequences. As I have suggested, American social and political theorists generally talk about civil rights as opposed to human rights. Indeed, counter-intuitively, American social and political theorists do not routinely employ the terminology of citizenship and citizen's rights. The principal, and I would say canonical, exception is Judith Shklar's *American Citizenship*, in which she claimed that "We are citizens only if we 'earn'".[5] For Shklar, working citizens are contrasted with slaves who have no rights as citizens and with aristocrats who, from the perspective of the Founding Fathers, have a predatory and parasitic relationship to civil society. By contrast, employment could never be a foundation of human rights, but it is, in my view, central to the idea of citizens as bearers of rights and duties.

Let me look more closely now at the absence (or at least underdevelopment) of a sociology of human rights. The reasons for this intellectual absence are diverse. As a discipline, sociology has been averse to general claims about universal institutions, concepts, and cultures. This reluctance to make general claims across societies and cultures is grounded in epistemological relativism. In attempting to fashion itself as an empirical science of society, sociology has largely turned its back on normative judgements on social institutions. Values, and the norms derived from values that operate in a given society, are merely the standards that ultimately happen to determine acceptable forms of behaviour. Such values and norms clearly vary from one society to another. Sociology is also (perhaps unofficially at least) committed to secularism and is suspicious of arguments that religious traditions and values have an independent effect on societies. It argues that the religion is, to use an expression from Marxist sociology, part of the superstructure and not causally independent. Within these secular presuppositions, any claim, which I examine shortly, that Christian ideas and values were influential in the rise of dignity as the core notion of human rights is merely wishful thinking.

There are some major exceptions to value-free secular assumptions in sociology. Leo Strauss, professor of political science at the University of Chicago (1949-1969), in *Natural Right and History* (1953) developed the most far-reaching criticism of this tradition with special reference to Max Weber, whose name is closely associated with the distinction between value relevance and value neutrality.[6] More recently, there has been a revival of interest in natural law in sociology that has inspired an interest in human rights. Philip Selznick defended the importance of natural law as a source of sociological understanding of common values.[7] Hans Joas in *The Sacredness of the Person* has sought to chart a course between the negative direction of relativism and self-defeating normative arguments.[8] His strategy is to counter secular accounts of the origins of human rights by demonstrating how key historical events contributed to the idea of human dignity and the universality of human values. Joas develops this argument via an engagement with, among others, Ernest Troeltsch and Georg Jellinek.[9] In *The Declaration of the Rights of Man and of Citizens: A Contribution to Modern Constitutional History* of 1895, Jellinek's objective was to uncover the early religious roots of human rights ideas and thereby to counter the standard view that it was the French Enlightenment that had been the fertile ground of "the rights of man and of citizens".[10] Jellinek treated the quest for freedom of religion as the original foundation of later claims for freedom of conscience in all matters of belief, both religious and secular. The other influence comes from Troeltsch, who also explored the religious and secular influences on the historical rise of rights in his "Stoic-Christian Natural Law and Modern Secular Law" in 1911.[11] Both writers were influential in the development of Weber's sociology of religion. However, Weber contributed more to the sociology of citizenship than to human rights in historical research on the city, his study of the Russian Revolution, and his assessment of the possibility of political reform in Germany after World War I.[12] While Weber's focus was on the impact of Protestantism on rights, Samuel Moyn has shown how Pope Pius XI in 1930 promoted the idea of human dignity.[13] The Pius XII's wartime Christian addresses announced basic universal human rights. Jacque Maritain was the Catholic philosopher who developed ideas about the person that shaped the core values and assumption behind the Declaration.

Despite the wealth of these contributions to our understanding of the origins of rights, these historical and philosophical considerations do not figure large in the mainstream sociological imagination. I take another example from the work of the American philosopher Richard Rorty who is examined carefully by Freeman. I admire the work of Rorty in *Achieving our Country*, for example.[14] His criticisms of relativism as self-refuting and his appreciation of the Judeo-Christian idea of dignity in "Postmodernist bourgeois liberalism" are important.[15] Rorty's argument can be treated as a form of consequentialism. Human rights are worthwhile (even if we can never agree on their definition), if the outcome of their enforcement is beneficial. Nevertheless, I find Rorty's minimalist view of rights and his argument regarding shared sentiments as a basis for human rights practice, as discussed by Freeman, too elementary and thin to be convincing or to have the practical outcomes he welcomes. By contrast, when sociologists have addressed the issue of rights, they have done so under the umbrella of the social rights of communities of citizens. Sociologists are likely to regard 'citizenship' as much richer and thicker than 'human rights'. For sociologists, 'citizenship' is part of a network of concepts and ideas that I call the 'C Words': city, citizenship, civilization, civil society, and civility. Weber and Jonas might add 'Christianity' or at least Protestant Christianity. What is the civility of the individual who is the subject of human rights?

In modern times, civility has somewhat lost its centrality to what we understand by the manners, comportment, and dispositions of an educated member of a civil society. For a sociologist like Edward Shils, civility included but was not exhausted by good behaviour. In *The Virtue of Civility*, he argued that norms of civility were critical to public debate in sustaining democratic institutions.[16] Civility involved respect for alternative and oppositional views and arguments, and was a fundamental component in the civilizing process of western societies from feudalism to liberal democracy.[17] It was a defence against the language of fascism with its simple binaries between the people or the folk and the intruders—communists, Jews, homosexuals. It was a critical aspect of democratic politics in which one engages with respect for arguments from opposed positions. Parliamentary democracy, for Shils, rests on civility as a defence against, in our times, fake news, abuse of public servants, death threats to people of opposing views, and general disrespect of others.[18] Civility and respect are necessary attributes of a successful civil society, but they are admittedly difficult to enforce. In Australia, we live in a period of incivility as a threat to citizenship and 'hard times' raise questions about the *quality* of political culture. Are we still as Australians in "the lucky country"?[19]

It is perhaps unsurprising that citizenship studies have flourished while engagement with human rights has remained a minority interest among sociologists. The critical publication was Thomas Marshall's *Citizenship and Social Class*.[20] He traced the growth of citizenship in the British Isles from the emergence of juridical norms and rights in the seventeenth century, such as *habeas corpus* and the jury system, the growth of political rights in the nineteenth century around the emergence of political parties, the reform of the electoral system, and the increasing importance of parliamentary democracy, and finally the development of social rights around insurance schemes, health care, and the welfare state in the twentieth century. Despite many criticisms and elaborations, his approach has survived. The sociology of citizenship has continued to expand with its own specialized journal, *Citizenship Studies*, and many edited collections such as the definitive *Oxford Handbook of Citizenship*.[21]

Can 'citizenship' solve the problems attending 'human rights'? The basic argument of this essay is that citizenship and human rights are different rights regimes and they are not easily reconciled. This may not be an original idea. Hans Joas neatly identified the central dilemma of any analysis of rights in *War and Modernity*: "the central conflict of values in this sphere today is the conflict between national sovereignty and the universalism of human rights".[22] In general terms, societies with legal systems that are explicitly founded on principles of national sovereignty, such as the United States, are resistant to legal pluralism. For this reason, they are also resistant to recognition of internal human rights law and are equally opposed to the development of Shari'a as a source of law in the United States. Although the Shari'a has been the dominant topic of legal pluralism, the same tensions exist around the recognition of the legal customs of aboriginal communities in white-settler societies. Although many societies have treaty agreements with native peoples, Australia still struggles to come to terms with the claims of its Aboriginal population.

There is consequently much confusion around the rights of citizens and the rights of human beings. What I take to be an ongoing contradiction was illustrated in 1789 by the French Revolution which spoke simultaneously about "the rights of man and the rights of the citizen". At least Edmund Burke, in *Reflections on the Revolution in France*, in 1790 was clear about the difference. For Burke, the rights of man were abstract, vague and flimsy by comparison with the (empirical) rights of an Englishman whose rights were based on tradition and custom. Institutions cannot be invented or legislated; they grow and evolve, responding to natural rather than artificial circumstances. He argued "it is with infinite caution that any man ought to venture upon pulling down an edifice which has answered in any tolerable degree for ages the common purposes of society, or building it up again without having models and patterns of approved utility before his eyes".[23] Burke treated 'natural rights' as sacred and hence not to be radically refashioned by revolutionary intervention.

Of course, Burke is often dismissed as a hopeless conservative and reactionary. He defended 'natural inequality' between people claiming that imposing equality on citizens in the French Revolution would destroy the natural order of society. While the revolutionary terror vindicated Burke's conservative criticism, he remains a controversial figure. We should however keep in mind that he was not opposed to natural rights. In his "Speech on Fox's East India Bill" in December 1781, he argued:

> The rights of men, that is to say, natural rights of mankind, are indeed sacred things; and if any public measure is proved mischievously to affect them, the objection ought to be fatal to that measure. . . . These things secured by these instruments may, without any deceitful ambiguity, be very fitly called the chartered rights of men.[24]

These natural rights are grounded in common historical experiences and rooted in civil society. They are not the abstract universal rights of the French Revolution. These rights of Englishmen are based on parliamentary practice and ultimately in the common law of the land. Burke was not opposed necessarily to revolution. After all, he celebrated the so-called Glorious Revolution of 1688. The monarchy had in fact upheld the constitution and the legal framework of liberty, but under George III had become corrupt. Thus, Burke did not reject the role of a landed aristocracy in creating a stable society, but he condemned the failure of political leadership that lay behind the American War of Independence. It was better, he argued, to grant America independence outright than to fight over it. In 1777, he wrote:

> I should expect ten times more benefit to this kingdom from the affection of America, though under a separate establishment, than from her perfect submission to the crown and parliament, accompanied with her terror, disgust, and abhorrence. Bodies tied together by so unnatural bond of union as mutual hatred, are only connected to their ruin.[25]

Why dwell on Burke? He is perhaps the starting point of any theory of national sovereignty that is based on a social contract that is designed, not so much to promote individual freedom, as to secure the public realm from civil violence and political instability. He formulated an early version of the idea that the common law better expresses the lived historical experience of a community of individuals than any abstract system of laws. At least one other reason for introducing Burke into this discussion is to prepare the way for a consideration of Hannah Arendt—one of the most important twentieth-century political thinkers on rights. Controversially, Hannah Arendt *appears* to have agreed with Burke in *The Origins of Totalitarianism*. She recognised that once the "transcendent measurements of religion or the law of nature have lost their authority", Hitler's slogan ("Right is what is good for the German people") is inescapable as a description of how the law operates. Consequently, these observations are "an ironical, bitter and belated confirmation" of Edmund Burke's political philosophy.[26] She went on to observe:

> The pragmatic soundness of Burke's concept seems to be beyond doubt in the light of our manifold experiences. Not only did loss of national rights in all instances entail the loss of human rights; the restoration of human rights, as the recent example of the State of Israel proves, has been achieved so far only through the restoration or establishment of national rights.[27]

Without citizenship, humans have no rights worth speaking of. Once the German Jews had lost their rights as citizens by legislative decree, they were deprived of their "right to have rights". They could not easily escape Germany because they had no valid passports or similar documents, and those that remained were exterminated because they had already, from a juridical perspective, ceased to exist. A similar argument can be applied to the suffering of the Rohingya community of Muslims are regarded as non-citizens by Myanmar's military rulers and hence unassimilable in a Buddhist state.

In this discussion so far, I have pitched social citizenship against human rights. We might say I have confronted the idea of dignity from Jacque Maritain (via Hans Jonas) with the common sense view of the empirical rights of an Englishman from Edmund Burke (via Hannah Arendt). However, neither citizenship nor human rights are static or ahistorical regimes of rights. Both are changing rapidly and in some respects are converging. Both are subject to the forces of globalisation which in some respects are driving them together rather than apart. In order to present this argument, I draw freely from Kate Nash's "Between Citizenship and Human Rights".[28] By contrast with Burke and Arendt, we live, especially in Australia, in a world that is profoundly shaped by globalisation and by the resulting inevitable growth of social and religious diversity. She begins her observations:

> Citizens belong to a bounded and exclusive political community with a shared history and prospective future. For the last 200 years, the basis of the common bound between citizens has been assumed to be the nation. . . Processes and discourses of globalization mean that questions of political participation which are framed in terms of the interests and values of citizens within separate and distinct nation-states are inappropriate where issues and events are not constrained within national territories . . . One of the most important aspects of globalization is the development of human rights'.[29]

In this argument, she follows Seyla Benhabib, for whom citizenship is becoming cosmopolitan, because human rights are no longer just moral norms.[30] They are becoming positive law that is attempting to regulate states, especially with regard to their treatment of immigrants, refugees, and asylum seekers. Through the delegated authority of the courts, human rights are increasingly legalised. However, from a sociological perspective, the enjoyment of rights cannot be simply a matter of formal legal entitlement, "it also depends on social structures through which power, material resources and meanings are created and circulated".[31] At the same time, a hierarchy of citizens is emerging with the growth of "frequent-flyer citizens" at the top.[32] Through their wealth, connections, and training, they are not tied to states and enjoy mobility across states. At lower levels, there are quasi-citizens such as guest workers, sub-citizens such as people waiting for their asylum status to be confirmed, and un-citizens or undocumented migrants and people incarcerated in 'non-places' such as Guantanamo Bay. In these circumstances, rights regimes are not working to equalize status differences within and between states.

Nash's critical unpacking of both social and human rights regimes is important and salutary. However, writing in 2009, we cannot blame her for not also recognising the political impact of those movements that currently challenge human rights, globalisation, and diversity in the name of 'the people', namely the movements that in general we label as 'populism'.[33] The globalisation of human rights' values and institutions is now radically challenged. Partly, this challenge is due to their association with the world of the elites who have benefitted most from the globalisation of capitalism versus those sectors, the lower middle and working class, that have benefitted least from economic growth. The greed of the elites is perceived as a moral affront to the austerity packages imposed on ordinary citizens as a consequence of the collapse of Lehman Brothers Holdings in 2008.[34] The challenge to elite greed has had a spectacular example in the Royal Commission into Misconduct in the Banking, Superannuation and Financial Services Industry, which disclosed not only greed but endless examples of incivility and disrespect towards citizens.[35]

What implications do these (often abstract) scholarly debates have for life in Australia in terms of its social and political (i.e. citizenship) rights and human rights? Australia has a score of 98/100 from the *Freedom in World Score* and has a specifically high rating for political and civil liberties. Our major cities are also successful in the *Global Cities Index* in which Sydney was ranked 15th and Melbourne 17th on four dimensions: personal well-being, economics, innovation and governance. However, Australia is constantly criticised, for example, in the *World Human Rights Report* (2019) for its "serious human rights issues" with special reference to refugee and asylum seekers who are confined on Manus Island in Papua New Guinea and in Nauru.[36] In terms of Indigenous rights, Aboriginals are over represented in the criminal justice system. There are also questions around disability rights where 50 per cent of the prison population suffer from some form of disability. Consequently, Indigenous and asylum practices continue to draw international condemnation. Can we measure citizenship?

Let us assume that protection of human and citizenship rights offers a measure of a successful society. There are various international measures that offer, sometimes indirectly, evidence relevant to answering the question—is a society successful? It is generally claimed that Australia has not suffered as traumatically as other societies from the decade-long economic crisis following the financial crisis of 2008-11. Australian banks had not been extensively exposed to imprudent lending practices and the housing market did not suffer the sub-prime crisis that affected the United States. There is also agreement that, provided the Chinese economy continues to grow, Australian exports will continue to be secure. Australia will remain the lucky country.

However, while these macro-changes may have been delayed in Australia, their negative consequences are now all too evident in the economy and society. For example, the closure of the car industry in Melbourne is a key illustration of the effects of economic globalisation. Deindustrialisation and the dangers of unregulated urban growth were fully recognised by the Morrison government in October 2018 with a proposal to limit population growth in Sydney and Melbourne.[37] There is general recognition that liberal-democratic governments have failed to deliver economic and political security by providing economic growth for all. In return, the people will no longer respect political elites on many key decisions shaping economic growth, national security, and democratic systems of governance. Extreme right-wing nationalist movements that threaten the security of minorities and migrants are one consequence of these macro transformations of economy and society, as was tragically illustrated by the terrorist attack on New Zealand mosques in March 2019. Despite their many limitations, human rights and citizenship are important legal and social mechanisms for promoting civility and social integration as valuable conditions for successful societies.

# Contributors

**Nicholas Aroney** is a professor of constitutional law at the University of Queensland, a fellow of the Centre for Law and Religion at Emory University, and an external member of the Islam, Law and Modernity research program at Durham University.

**Terri Butler** is the member for Griffith in the Parliament of the Commonwealth of Australia.

**Michael Casey** is the director of Australian Catholic University's public policy think-tank, the PM Glynn Institute.

**Jennifer Cook** is the general counsel of the Catholic Archdiocese of Sydney.

**Emma Dawson** is the executive director of the public policy think-tank Per Capita.

**Damien Freeman** is the editor of the Kapunda Press at the PM Glynn Institute.

**Catherine Renshaw** is a professor of law at Western Sydney University and a fellow of the PM Glynn Institute.

**Bryan Turner** is a professor of sociology at Australian Catholic University, an emeritus professor at the Graduate Center, City University of New York, and a member of the Academy of the Social Sciences in Australia.

**Tim Wilson** is the member for Goldstein in the Parliament of the Commonwealth of Australia and formerly served as Australia's Human Rights Commissioner.

# Notes

### Prologue: The end of human rights?

1. H. Arendt, "Understanding Politics (The Difficulties of Understanding)" in J. Kohn (ed.), *Essays in Understanding 1930-54* (Harcourt, Brace & Co, 1994), p. 318.
2. "Consensus Statement on Conscientious Objection in Healthcare", 29 August 2016: <http://blog.practicalethics.ox.ac.uk/2016/08/consensus-statement-on-conscientious-objection-in-healthcare/>.
3. A. Giubilini and F. Minerva, "After-birth abortion: why should the baby live?", *Journal of Medical Ethics*, Vol. 39, pp. 261-63.
4. *Ibid.*, p. 262.
5. *Ibid.*, p. 263
6. I am grateful to Damien Freeman and Professor Catherine Renshaw for observations they made in discussing the ideas in this prologue with me, and to Fr Frank Brennan SJ and Professor Hayden Ramsay for comments and suggestions they offered on the draft text.

### Introduction: rights, nonsense and the commentariat

1. *Nationwide News Pty Ltd v Wills* (1992) 177 CLR 1.
2. C. Renshaw, "National Human Rights Institutions and Civil Society Organizations: New Dynamics of Engagement at Domestic, Regional, and International Levels", *Global Governance*, Vol. 18(3), 2012, p. 299.
3. *National Human Rights Consultation Report*, September 2009.

### In the long grass

1. P. Larkin, "The Mower" from *Collected Poems* (Farrar Straus and Giroux, 2001).
2. R. Rorty, "Human Rights, Rationality, and Sentimentality" in S. Shute and S. Hurley (eds), *On Human Rights: Oxford Amnesty Lectures 1993* (Basic Books, 1993), pp. 111-34.
3. D. Rieff, "Letter from Bosnia", *New Yorker*, 23 November 1992, pp. 82-95 (as cited by Rorty, p. 112).
4. Rorty, *op. cit.*, p. 118.
5. *Ibid.*, pp. 118-19.
6. *Ibid.*, p. 122.
7. *Ibid.*, pp. 122-23
8. *Ibid.*, p. 127.

9   "Human Rights: A Very Bad Idea", Interview of Raymond Geuss by Lawrence Hamilton for *Theoria: A Journal of Social and Political Theory*, Vol. 60(2), June 2013, pp. 83-102.
10  *Ibid.*, p. 92
11  *Ibid.*
12  *Ibid.*, p. 90
13  *Ibid.*
14  *Ibid.*, p. 91
15  *Ibid.*
16  *Ibid.*, pp. 97-98
17  *Ibid.*, p. 90
18  *Ibid.*, p. 89
19  *Ibid.*, p. 92
20  *Ibid.*, p. 93
21  This is not the occasion for an extended discussion of these theorists, but the relevant positions may be found in Charles de Montesquieu, *The Spirit of the Laws*, ed. A. M. Cohler, B. C. Miller and H. S. Stone (Cambridge University Press, 1989 [1748]); A. V. Dicey, *Introduction to the Study of the Law of the Constitution*, 8th edn (Macmillan, 1915); W. I. Jennings, *The Law and the Constitution* (University of London Press, 1959); W. Bagehot, *The English Constitution* (Chapman and Hall, 1867).
22  J. Leeser MP, "Human Rights Hijacked", 2018 B'nai B'rith Human Rights Address, Emanuel Synagogue, Woollahra, 15 July 2018. The speech is available at <www.julianleeser.com.au>.

## Where the light gets in

1   *Quartz*, "Light in the Dark", available at: <https://qz.com/835076/leonard-cohens-anthem-the-story-of-the-line-there-is-a-crack-in-everything-thats-how-the-light-gets-in/>.
2   S. Hopgood, *The Endtimes of Human Rights* (Cornell University Press, 2013); E. A. Posner, *The Twilight of Human Rights Law* (Oxford University Press, 2014); S. Moyn, *The Last Utopia: Human Rights in History* (Harvard University Press, 2010).
3   B. Simmons, *Mobilizing for Human Rights* (Cambridge University Press, 2009); J. Brunee and S. J. Toope, *Legitimacy and Legality in International Law* (Cambridge University Press, 2010); T. Risse, S. C. Ropp and K. Sikkink (eds), *The Power of Human Rights: International Norms and Domestic Change* (Cambridge University Press, 1999); T. Risse, S. C. Ropp and K. Sikkink (eds), *The Persistent Power of Human Rights: From Commitment to Compliance* (Cambridge University Press, 2013); H. Koh, "How Is International Human Rights Law Enforced?", *Indiana Law Journal*, Vol. 74(4), 1999, pp. 1396, 1397–1398.
4   E. Hafner‐Burton and K. Tsutsui, "Human Rights in a Globalizing World: The Paradox of Empty Promises", *American Journal of Sociology*, Vol. 110(5), 2005, p. 1373; E. Hafner-Burton and K. Tsutsui, "Justice Lost! The Failure of International Human Rights Law to Matter Where Needed Most", *Journal of Peace Research*, Vol. 44(4), 2007, p. 407.
5   J. Raz, "Human Rights without Foundations" in S. Besson and J. Tasioulas (eds), *The Philosophy of International Law* (Oxford University Press, 2010), p. 321.
6   J. Griffin, *On Human Rights* (Oxford University Press, 2009), p. 248; A. Gewirth, "The

basis and content of human rights" in J. R. Pennock and J. W. Chapman (eds), *Human Rights, Nomos XXIII* (New York University Press, 1981), p. 119.

7   Raz, *op. cit.*

8   H. Lauterpacht, *International Law and Human Rights* (Stevens, 1950).

9   For a discussion of the different accounts, see: P. Slotte and M. Halme-Tuomisaari (eds), *Revisiting the Origins of Human Rights* (Cambridge University Press, 2015), pp. 3-6. A third account sees the 'true' beginning of the modern human rights movement in the 1970s. See Moyn, *op. cit.*

10  C. Beitz, *The Idea of Human Rights* (Oxford University Press, 2009). Beitz and others have answered the question about the nature of human rights by developing what has come to be known as 'political' accounts of human rights. See: K. Baynes, "Discourse ethics and the political conception of human rights", *Ethics and Global Politics*, Vol. 2(1), 2009, p. 1

11  S. Jones, "Human Rights in Diverse Cultures" in S. Caney and P. Jones (eds), *Human Rights and Global Diversity* (Frank Cass Publishers, 2001), p. 34.

12  M. Mutua, *Human Rights: A Political and Cultural Critique* (University of Pennsylvania Press, 2002); J. Cobbah, "African Values and the Human Rights Debate: An African Perspective", *Human Rights Quarterly*, Vol. 9, 1987, p. 309; C. Ake "The African Context of Human Rights", *Africa Today*, Vol. 34, 1987, p. 5; J. Chan, "Human Rights and Confucian Virtues", *Harvard Asia Quarterly*, Vol. 4, 2000, p. 51.

13  M. Mutua, "Savages, victims, and saviors: the metaphor of human rights", *Harvard International Law Journal*, Vol. 42(1), 2001, p. 201, 208.

14  UNGA, World Conference on Human Rights, Vienna Declaration and Programme of Action, A/CONF.157/23 (25 June 1993), Article 5.

15  R. Rorty, "Human Rights, Rationality, and Sentimentality" in R. Rorty, *Truth and Progress: Philosophical Papers* (Cambridge University Press, 1998), Vol. 3, p. 167.

16  T. Nagel, "Personal Rights and Public Space" in H. H. Koh and R. C. Slye (eds), *Deliberative Democracy and Human Rights* (Yale University Press, 1999), pp. 33-48, 34.

17  J. Donnelly, "Human rights and human dignity: An analytic critique of non-Western conceptions of human rights", *American Political Science Review*, Vol. 76(2), 1982, p. 303.

18  L. Marasinghe, "Traditional Conceptions of Human Rights in Africa" in C. E. Welch, Jr. and R. I. Meltzer (eds), *Human Rights and Development in Africa* (State University of New York Press, 1984), pp. 32-45, 43. For a different view see: A. Pollis and P. Schwab, "Human Rights: A Western Construct with Limited Applicability" in A. Pollis and P. Schwab (eds), *Human Rights: Cultural and Ideological Perspectives* (Praeger Publishers, 1979), pp. 1, 15.

19  T. Nagel, *op. cit.*, pp. 33-48, 34.

20  C. Taylor, "Conditions of an Unforced Consensus on Human Rights" in J. E. Bauer and D. A. Bell (eds), *The East Asian Challenge for Human Rights* (Cambridge University Press, 1999), pp. 124-146, p. 126.

21  B. Williams, "In the Beginning was the Deed" in *Deliberative Democracy and Human Rights*, above, p. 145.

22  J. Rawls, *The Law of Peoples* (Harvard University Press, 1999), p. 65.

23  International Covenant on Civil and Political Rights (adopted 16 December 1966, 999 UNTS 171, entered into force 3 November 1976).

24 P. Carozza, *op. cit.*, p. 303.
25 J. Ching, "Human Rights: A Valid Chinese Concept?" in W. M. T. de Bary and T. Weiming (eds), *Confucianism and Human Rights* (Columbia University Press, 1998), p. 70-71.
26 J. Chan, "An Alternative View", *Journal of Democracy*, Vol. 8(2), 1997, p. 35. See also: J. Cohen, "Minimalism About Human Rights: The Most We Can Hope For?", *Journal of Political Philosophy*, Vol. 12(2), 2004, p. 190, 203.
27 O. Yasuaki, "Towards an Intercivilizational Approach to Human Rights" in *The East Asian Challenge for Human Rights*, n. 20 above, pp. 103-124, 109.
28 Examples commonly given of the contested scope of core rights are abortion and infanticide, in the context of the right to life. Abortion is at present legal in most Western countries: Centre for Reproductive Rights "The World's Abortion Laws" available at: <http://worldabortionlaws.com/map/>. In ancient Greece, Plato and Aristotle supported infanticide in cases of weak or deformed infants who might be a burden on the state: B. R. Sharma, "Historical and Medico-legal Aspects of Infanticide: an Overview", *Medicine, Science and the Law*, Vol. 46(2), 2006, p. 152.
29 J. Waldron, "Dignity, Rights, and Responsibilities", *Arizona State Law Journal*, Vol. 43, 2011, p. 1107.
30 T. Nagel, *op. cit.*
31 R. Panikkar, "Is the Notion of Human Rights a Western Concept?", *Diogenes*, Vol. 30, 1982, p. 75, 79.
32 J. Rawls, "The Law of Peoples", *Critical Inquiry*, Vol.20(1), 1993, p. 36; M. Ignatieff, *Human Rights as Politics and as Idolatry* (Princeton University Press, 2001); C. Beitz, "Human Rights and the Law of Peoples" in D. Chatterjee (ed), *The Ethics of Assistance* (Cambridge University Press, 2004); J. Cohen, "Minimalism about Human Rights: the Most We Can Hope For?", *Journal of Political Philosophy*, Vol. 12(2), 2004, p. 190, 203; P. Jones, "International Human Rights: Political or Metaphysical?" in S. Caney, D. George and P. Jones (eds) *National Rights, International Obligations* (Boulder, CO, Westview, 1996), pp. 183–204.
33 Jacques Maritain, United Nations Educational, Social and Cultural Organization (UNESCO) (ed), *Human Rights Comments and Interpretations: A Symposium* (1949) New York, Columbia University Press, 17.
34 Cited in M. A. Glendon, *A World Made New: Eleanor Roosevelt and the Universal Declaration of Human Rights* (Random House, 2001).
35 Beitz, *op. cit.*, n. 10.
36 *Ibid.*
37 Bayne, *op. cit.*
38 J. Rawls, *The Law of Peoples, op. cit.*, n. 10; Beitz, *op. cit.*; Raz, *op. cit.*; J. Cohen, "Is There a Human Right to Democracy?" in C. Syprowich (ed), *The Egalitarian Conscience: Essays in Honour of G.A. Cohen* (Oxford University Press, 2006), pp. 226–248, 238.
39 This idea brings together the work of Rainer Forst and Seyla Benhabib—who (in different ways) follow Habermas's discourse ethics in arguing that the form that rights take must be determined discursively by those affected through speech acts demanding recognition; and the work of proponents of political theories of human rights (John Rawls, Charles Beitz, Joshua Cohen). See, for example, K. Baynes, *op. cit.*, pp. 1-21.
40 A. Schaap, "Enacting the Rights to have Rights: Jacques Ranciere's critique of Hannah Arendt", *European Journal of Political Theory*, 2011, pp. 22-45.
41 John Howard, Doorstop Interview, Darwin. Accessed 5 August, 2003: <www.pm.gov.

au/news/interviews/Interview406.html>.
42 L. McKenny, "Same-sex marriage could lead to polygamy, says Jensen", *The Sydney Morning Herald*, 11 June, 2011.
43 R. Gaita, "Same-Sex Marriage: A Philosophical Perspective": <http://www.lamonash.edu.au/castancentre/public-edu/gaita-ssm.html>.
44 Peter Wildeblood, *Against the Law* (2nd ed) (Penguin, 1957), p. 8.
45 *Ibid*.
46 Lord Devlin, *The Enforcement of Morals* (Oxford University Press, 1959), p. 7.
47 *Ibid*.
48 R. Dworkin, "Lord Devlin and the enforcement of morals", *Yale Law Journal*, 1966, p. 986.
49 *ibid*.
50 op.cit., p. 17.
51 Dworkin, *op. cit.*, p. 992.
52 UDHR, article 29.
53 Ninth International Conference of American States, American Declaration on the Rights and Duties of Man, Bogota, Colombia (2 May 1948). Preamble. There is also a special section in the American Declaration which emphasises specific duties: to society; towards children and parents; to vote; to acquire an elementary education; to obey the law; to cooperate with the state and the community with respect to social security and welfare; to pay taxes; to work: Ch. 2, arts, XXIX-XXXVIII.
54 American Convention on Human Rights (adopted 22 November 1969, 1144 UNTS 143, entered into force 18 July 1978). Art 32(1). The Preamble to the International Covenant on Civil and Political Rights also recognises duties:

> the individual . . . is under a responsibility to strive for the promotion and observance of the rights recognized in the present Covenant . . . Such private duties and responsibilities cannot be fulfilled if an individual violates the rights of other individuals or groups, and the preamble to the Covenant clearly states that, with respect to human rights, individuals have 'duties to other individuals'.

55 African Charter on Human and Peoples' Rights (Banjul Charter) (adopted 27 June 1981, 1520 UNTS 217, entered into force 21 October 1986). The Preamble recognizes "that the enjoyment of rights and freedoms also implies the performance of duties on the part of everyone," and Articles 27–29 of the Charter contain specific duties of individuals.
56 J. J. Paust, "The Other Side of Right: Private Duties under Human Rights Law", *Harvard Human Rights Journal*, Vol. 5, 1992, pp. 51, 62.
57 B. Saul, "In the Shadow of Human Rights: Human Duties, Obligations and Responsibilities", *Columbia Human Rights Law Review*, Vol. 32, 2000, p. 565.
58 Y. Ghai, "Human Rights and Governance: the Asia Debate", *Asia-Pacific Journal of Human Rights and the Law*, Vol. 1, 2000, pp. 9, 33.
59 *Ibid*.
60 N. Englehart, "Rights and Culture in the Asian Values Argument: the Rise and Fall of Confucian Ethics in Singapore", *Human Rights Quarterly*, Vol. 22(2), 2000, p. 548.
61 J. Waldron, "Rights in Conflict", *Ethics*, Vol. 99(3), 1989, p. 503.

62  J. Raz, *The Morality of Freedom* (Clarendon, 1986), p. 166.
63  A. Sen, "Elements of a Theory of Human Rights", *Philosophy & Public Affairs*, Vol. 32(4), 2004, p. 315.
64  T. Pogge, "Cosmopolitanism and Sovereignty", *Ethics*, Vol. 103(1), 1992, p. 48.
65  M. A. Glendon, "Knowing the Universal Declaration of Human Rights", *op. cit.*
66  R. Forst, *The Basic Right to Justification* (Constellations, 1999), p. 42.

## 1. The use and usefulness of human rights in our parliament

1  Those instruments include the International Convention on the Elimination of all Forms of Racial Discrimination, the International Covenant on Economic, Social and Cultural Rights, the International Covenant on Civil and Political Rights, the Convention on the Elimination of All Forms of Discrimination Against Women, the Convention Against Torture and Other Cruel, Inhuman or Degrading Treatment or Punishment, the Convention on the Rights of the Child, and the Convention on the Rights of Persons with Disabilities.
2  Australian Senate, Select Committee on the Exposure Draft of the Marriage Amendment (Same-Sex Marriage) Bill, *Report on the Commonwealth Government's Exposure Draft of the Marriage Amendment (Same-Sex Marriage) Bill*, 15 February 2017.
3  P. Gregoire, Interview with Michael Kirby on 8 September 2017 for Sydney Criminal Lawyer blog: <https://www.sydneycriminallawyers.com.au/blog/marriage-equality-an-interview-with-former-high-court-justice-michael-kirby/>.
4  E. Burke, "Speech to the Electors of Bristol", 3 November 1774, in his *Works*, Vol. 1, pp. 446-48.
5  Australian Senate, Standing Orders, Standing Order No. 24.
6  On 1 September 2016, the Minister, the Hon. Christopher Pyne MP issued the Parliamentary Joint Committee on Human Rights Appointment: <https://www.aph.gov.au/Parliamentary_Business/Committees/Joint/Human_Rights/>.
7  I am grateful to Damien Freeman and to Georgia Betros for their comments on earlier drafts of this essay.

## 2. A constant conversation

1  H. Collins, "Political ideology in Australia: the distinctiveness of a Benthamite Society" in S. R. Graubard (ed), *Australia: the Daedalus Symposium* (Angus and Robertson, 1985), Vol. 114, pp 147–169.
2  *Ibid.*
3  *Ibid.*
4  D. Kemp, *The Liberals: A Short history of liberalism in Victoria and Australia* (2009).
5  Australian Constitution, section 116.
6  *Ibid.*, section 51 (xxxi).
7  I. Berlin, "Two concepts of liberty" in *Four Essays on Liberty* (Oxford University Press, 1969), pp 118-172.

8   *Ibid.*
9   *Ibid.*
10  *Ibid.*
11  M. Nowak, *U.N. Covenant on Civil and Political Rights CCPR Commentary*, 2nd edn (Engel, 2005), p. 439.
12  *Ibid.*
13  K. Alston, *Freedom of Expression and school dress codes: South African and international perspectives* (University of Fort Hare, 2006), pp. 83-94.
14  R. Schmidt-McCleave, "The "haircut case" – what was it really about" (Auckland District Law Society, 2014): <https://www.adls.org.nz/for-the-profession/news-and-opinion/2014/8/15/the-%E2%80%9Chaircut-case%E2%80%9D-%E2%80%93-what-was-it-really-about/>.
15  "Australia's Human Rights Framework", Department of Attorney-General, Commonwealth of Australia, 2010, p. 8: <https://www.ag.gov.au/Consultations/Documents/Publicsubmissionsonthedraftbaselinestudy/AustraliasHumanRightsFramework.pdf>.
16  J. Leeser, "Human rights hijacked", 2018 B'nai B'rith Human Rights Address, 15 July, 2018: <https://www.julianleeser.com.au/media/speeches/human-rights-hijacked-2018-bnai-brith-human-rights-address>.
17  "National Human Rights Consultation: Report" (Attorney General's Department, 09/2009), Commonwealth of Australia, p. 43.

## 3. Disagreeing about rights and interests

1   R. Geuss, History and Illusion in Politics (Cambridge University Press, 2001).
2   "Human Rights: A Very Bad Idea", Interview of Raymond Geuss by Lawrence Hamilton for *Theoria: A Journal of Social and Political Theory*, Vol. 60(2), 2013, p. 84.

## 4. Our common lives

*No notes*

## 5. Splitting our differences

1   M. A. Glendon, *Rights Talk: The Impoverishment of Political Discourse* (The Free Press, 1991), p. 173.
2   *Ibid.*, p. 8.
3   C. Sunstein, "Rights and Their Critics" *Notre Dame Law Review*, vol. 70, 1995, extract found in H. Steiner and P. Alston, *International Human Rights in Context: Law, Politics and Morals*, 2nd edn (Oxford University Press, 2000), p. 335.

4   E. Kamenka, "Human Rights, Peoples' Rights" in J. Crawford (ed), *The Rights of Peoples* (Clarendon Press, 1988), p. 127; extract found in Steiner and Alston, p. 330; and Sunstein, *op. cit.*, p. 334.
5   L. Chappell, J. Chesterman, and L. Hill, *The Politics of Human Rights* (Cambridge University Press, 2009), p. 1.
6   Glendon, preface.
7   *op. cit.*
8   Glendon, p. 176, pp. 34 and 41, n. 10.
9   Glendon, *op. cit.*, p. 176; see also "Michael Ignatieff's Critique of Human Rights (and other Scenes from the National Humanities Center)", 10 June 2014, at <http://humanityjournal.org/blog/michael-ignatieffs-critique-of-human-rights-and-other-scenes-from-the-national-humanities-center/>.
10  J. Waldron (ed), *'Nonsense Upon Stilts': Bentham, Burke and Marx on the Rights of Man* (Methuen & Co, 1987), p. 164.
11  *Ibid.*, p. 165.
12  Glendon, *op. cit.*, pp. 180-81.
13  *Ibid.*, p. 179.
14  D. Clément "Human rights or social justice? The problem of rights inflation", *The International Journal of Human Rights*, vol. 22(2), 2018, pp. 155-169, p. 158.
15  See Freedom Rights Project website: <http://www.freedomrights.info/activities/new-frp-report-1377-human-rights/#>; see also Clément, *op. cit.*, p. 155.
16  Sunstein, *op. cit.*; see also Clément, *op. cit.*, p. 155.
17  Clément, *op. cit.*, p. 156.
18  Freedom Rights Project at <http://www.freedomrights.info/activities/new-frp-report-1377-human-rights/#>.
19  Clément, *op. cit.*, pp. 156 and 164; see also D. Clement, "Human Rights Inflation: Why the International Human Rights Regime Risks Impoverishing Liberty", conference of the Henry Jackson Society, held 16 July 2013 at House of Commons, London, see <https://henryjacksonsociety.org/2013/07/16/human-rights-inflation-why-the-international-human-rights-regime-risks-impoverishing-liberty-2/>.
20  Clément, *op. cit.*, n. 14., p. 164.
21  Glendon, *op. cit.*, preface.
22  B. Saul, "The Light of Human Rights is Fading in Australia," ABC News online, 7 October 2014: <https://www.abc.net.au/news/2014-10-07/saul-the-light-of-human-rights-is-fading-in-australia/5794640>.
23  Chappell et al, *op. cit.*, p. 49.
24  Chappell et al, *op. cit.*, p. 50.
25  *Ibid.*, p. 55.
26  J. Hewson, "Frydenberg Looks Ridiculous as Government Gets into a Pickle", *Sydney Morning Herald*, 10 April 2019.
27  Chappell et al, *op. cit.*, p. 55.
28  A. Bogle, "Laws Targeting Terror Videos on Facebook and YouTube 'Rushed' and 'Knee-Jerk', Lawyers and Tech Industry Say", ABC Science, 4 April 2019: <https://

www.abc.net.au/news/science/2019-04-04/facebook-youtube-social-media-laws-rushed-and-flawed-critics-say/10965812>: see also A. Tillett, Y. Redrup, and M. Mason, "Kicking Us While We're Down: Atlassian Chief Savages New Terror Laws", *Australian Financial Review*, 4 April 2019.

29  Tillett et al, *op. cit.*, p. 28.
30  P. J. Deneen, *Why Liberalism Failed* (Yale University Press, 2018), pp. 192-195.
31  Chappell et al, *op. cit.*, p. 2.
32  *Ibid.*, p. 22.
33  *Ibid.*, p. 22, citing H. Charlesworth, *Writing in Rights: Australia and the Protection of Human Rights*. (UNSW Press, 2002), p. 39, and G. Williams "Five Reasons to Rewrite the Constitution" in G. Patmore and G. Jungworth (eds), *The Big Makeover: A New Constitution: Labor Essays* (Pluto Press, 2002), p. 43.
34  R. Gittens, "Why Politicians Only Pretend to Care about Low Income Earners," *Sydney Morning Herald*, 10 April 2019.
35  Chappell et al, *op. cit.*, p. 71, citing Charlesworth.
36  *Ibid.*, p. 71, citing F. Brennan, *Acting on Conscience: How can we responsibly mix law, religion and politics?* (University of Queensland Press, 2007), p. 123.
37  J. Ferguson, "Bishops Turn Poll Spotlight on to Plight of Indigenous", *The Australian*, 17 April 2019; See also Australian Catholic Bishops' press release at <https://www.catholic.org.au/acbc-media/media-centre/media-releases-new/2185-bishops-call-for-politics-that-promote-peace-common-good/file>, and the Bishops' full election statement at <https://www.catholic.org.au/acbc-media/media-centre/media-releases-new/2186-election-statement-politics-in-service-of-peace/file>.
38  Chappell et al, *op. cit.*, p. 32, citing C. Saunders, "Protecting Rights in Common Law Constitutional Systems: A Framework for A Comparative Study", *Victoria University Wellington Law Review*, vol. 33, 2002, pp. 83-112, p. 104.
39  Chappell et al, *op. cit.*, pp. 29-30.
40  *Ibid.*, p. 36.
41  *Ibid.*, p. 53; see also p. 43.
42  *Ibid.*, p. 63; see also p. 57.
43  *Ibid.*, p. 74.
44  *Ibid.*, p. 78.
45  S. Moulds, "It is Time To Talk About Rights Protection In South Australia", *In Daily*, 1 March 2019: <https://indaily.com.au/opinion/2019/03/01/its-time-to-talk-about-rights-protection-in-south-australia/>.
46  Chappell et al, *op. cit.*, p. 81, citing S. Evans and C. Evans, "Australian Parliaments and the Protection of Human rights", *Papers on Parliament*, no 47, (Canberra: Department of the Senate, 2007).
47  Glendon, *op. cit.*, p. 176, citing S. Macedo, *Liberal Virtues* (Clarendon Press, 1990), p. 71.

## 6. Human rights versus citizenship

1. B. S. Turner, "Sociology of Human Rights" in D. Shelton (ed), *The Oxford Handbook of Human Rights* (Oxford University Press, 2013), pp.82-103.
2. B. S. Turner, "The erosion of citizenship", *British Journal of Sociology*, vol. 52(2), 2001, pp. 189-209.
3. D. Lyons, "The correlativity of rights and duties", *Nous* vol. 4(1), 1970, pp. 45-55.
4. E. F. Isin and G. M. Nielsen (eds), *Acts of Citizenship* (Chicago University Press, 2008).
5. A. Shachar, R. Baubock, I. Bloemraad, and M. Vink (eds), *The Oxford Handbook of Citizenship* (Oxford University Press, 2017), p. 67.
6. L. Strauss, *Natural Right and History* (University of Chicago Press, 1953).
7. P. Selznick, "Sociology of Natural Law", *The American Journal of Jurisprudence*, vol. 6(1), 1961, pp. 84-108.
8. H. Joas, *The Sacredness of the Person: a new genealogy of human rights* (Georgetown University Press, 2013).
9. H. Joas, "The Independence of Religious Phenomena: The Work of Ernst Troeltsch as a Template for the Study of Religion" in C. Adair-Toteff (ed), *The Anthem Companion to Ernst Troeltsch* (Anthem Press, 2018), pp. 25-36.
10. G. Jellinek, *Die Erklarung der Menschen und Burgerrechte. Ein Beitrag zur modernen Verfassungsgeschichte.* (Munich and Leipzig, 1895).
11. E. Troeltsch, "Stoic-Christian Natural Law and Modern Secular Law" in C. Adair-Toteff (ed.), *Sociological Beginnings: The First Conference of the German Society for Sociology* (Liverpool University Press, 1991), pp. 110-131.
12. D. Kelly, "Max Weber and the Rights of Citizens", *Max Weber Studies*, vol. 4(1), 2004, pp. 23-49.
13. S. Moyn, *The Last Utopia: Human Rights in History* (The Belknap Press, 2015).
14. R. Rorty, *Achieving Our Country* (Harvard University Press, 1998).
15. R. Rorty, "Postmodern bourgeois liberalism" in *Objectivity, Relativism, and Truth* (Cambridge University Press, 1991), pp. 197-202.
16. E. Shils, *The Virtue of Civility* (Liberty Fund, 1997).
17. N. Elias, *The Civilizing Process. The History of Manners* (Blackwell, 1939).
18. B. Harcourt, "The Politics of Incivility", *Arizona Law Review*, vol. 54, 2012, pp. 345-374.
19. D. Horne, *The Lucky Country* (Penguin Books, 1964).
20. T. H. Marshall, *Citizenship and Social Class* (Cambridge University Press, 1950).
21. A. Shachar, B. Ayelet, R. Bauboeck, I. Bloemraad, and M. Vink (eds) *The Oxford Handbook of Citizenship* (Oxford University Press, 2017).
22. J. Hans, *War and Modernity* (Polity Press, 2003), p. 23.
23. E. Burke, *Reflections on the Revolution in France* (The Liberal Arts Press, 1955), p. 70.
24. E. Burke, "Speech on Fox's East India Bill" (1783) in J. Norman (ed.), *Reflections on the Revolution in France and Other Writings* (Everyman's Library [Alfred A. Knopf], 2017), p. 371.
25. E. Burke, "A Letter to the Sheriffs of Bristol on the Affairs of America" (1777) in A. J.George (ed.), *Edmund Burke: Speeches on the American War* (D. C. Heath & Co. Library of

the University of California), vol. II, p. 36.
26 H. Arendt, *The Origins of Totalitarianism*. (San Diego: Harcourt, 1968), p. 299.
27 *Ibid.*
28 K. Nash, "Between Citizenship and Human Rights", *Sociology*, vol. 43(6), 2009, pp. 1067-1083.
29 *Ibid.*, pp. 1067 and 1068.
30 S. Benhabib, *The Rights of Others: Aliens, Residents and Citizens* (Cambridge University Press, 2004).
31 Nash, *op. cit.*, p. 1069.
32 C. Calhoun, "The Class Consciousness of Frequent Travellers: Towards a Critique of Actually Existing Cosmopolitanism" in D. Archibugi (ed.), *Debating Cosmopolitics* (Verso, 2003), pp. 86-116.
33 G. Fitzi, J. Mackert and B. S. Turner (eds), *Populism and the Crisis of Democracy* (Routledge, 2019) 3 volumes.
34 A. Shipman, J. Edmunds and B. S. Turner, *The New Power Elite. Inequality, Politics and Greed* (Anthem Press, 2018).
35 K. H. Hayne, *Royal Commission into Misconduct in the Banking, Superannuation and Financial Services Industry* (2018).
36 *World Human Rights Report* (2019), *Human Rights Watch 29th Report*.
37 "Biggest cities off limits for some new migrants", *The Australian*, 9 October 2018.
38 *Ibid.*

# Index

Aquinas, St Thomas 3
Arendt, Hannah x, 117-118

Bagehot, Walter 28
Bayne, Peter 48
Beitz, Charles 48
Benhabib, Seyla 118, 126 (n 39)
Bentham, Jeremy 2-3, 66, 70, 72, 74
Berlin, Sir Isaiah 76
Bligh, William 75
Brennan, Frank 81, 105
Burke, Edmund 1, 26, 65, 72, 93, 115-118
Burney, Linda 105

Casey, M.A. 38, 100-101
Chappell, Louise 98, 105-106
Charlesworth, Hilary 105
Chesterman, John 98, 105-106
Chichele, Henry 14
Clément, Dominique 101
Cohen, Leonard 41
Collins, Hugh 74
Confucius 45
Cunliffe, Fossie 14

Deneen, Patrick 104
Devlin, Patrick, Baron 51-53
Dicey, A.V. 28
Dworkin, Ronald 52-53

Folau, Israel 94
Forst, Rainer 57, 126 (n 39)
Freeman, Damien 63, 67, 70, 81-88, 91-93, 97-98, 100, 107, 109, 113

Gaita, Raimond 50
Gandhi, Mahatma 54
George III, King 116
George VI, King 14
Geuss, Raymond 22-26, 70, 84, 87
Ghai, Yash 55, 94
Gittens, Ross 105
Glendon, Mary Ann 56, 96-99, 101
Gwyer, Sir Maurice 14

Habermas, Jürgen 126 (n 39)
Halévy, Elie 74
Hamilton, Lawrence 84
Hart, H.L.A. 51-52
Hewson, John 103
Hill, Lisa 98, 105-106
Hitler, Adolf 117
Homer 14-15
Howard, J.W. 49, 103
Hume, David 75

Ignatieff, Michael 47
Isin, Engin 110

Jellinek, Georg 112
Jennings, Sir Ivor 28
Jensen, Peter 49
Joas, Hans 112-114, 117

Kant, Immanuel 3, 20
Kemp, David 75
Kirby, Michael 65, 72

Lang, Cosmo Gordon 14
Larkin, Philip 19-21, 83

Leeser, Julian 26, 29-38, 67, 79, 84-89, 109
Locke, John 75
Lockhart, J.G. 14

Maritain, Jacque 47, 113, 117
Marshall, Thomas 114
Mencius 45
Montagu of Beaulieu, Edward, 3rd Baron 50
Montesquieu, Charles de 28, 75
Moses, Arthur 104
Moulds, Sarah 107
Moyn, Sam 112
Mutua, Makau 43

Nagel, Thomas 44
Nash, Kate 118-119
Nowak, Manfred 77

Paine, Thomas 1-2
Palda, Karel 15
Pannikar, Raimon 46-47
Parks, Rosa 48, 110
Paust, Jordan J. 55
PittRivers, Michael 50
Pius XII, Pope 112
Plato 20-21
Pogge, Thomas 56

Rawls, John 45, 48
Raz, Joseph 56
Renshaw, Catherine 63, 70-71, 80, 88-89, 94-95, 102, 107, 109-110
Rieff, David 20
Rorty, Richard 20-22, 25, 44, 84, 113

Saul, Ben 55, 102
Saunders, Cheryl 105

Selznick, Philip 112
Sen, Amartya 56
Shils, Edward 113-114
Shklar, Judith 111
Smith, Adam 75
Steel-Maitland, Sir Arthur 14
Strauss, Leo 112
Sunstein, Cass 100

Taylor, Charles 45
Toonen, Nicholas 102
Troeltsch, Ernest 112

Waldron, Jeremy 99
Weber, Max 112-113
Wilbrahim, Sir Philip 14
Wildeblood, Peter, 50
Williams, Bernard 45

Yasuaki, Onuma 45

www.ingramcontent.com/pod-product-compliance
Ingram Content Group UK Ltd.
Pitfield, Milton Keynes, MK11 3LW, UK
UKHW021326180426
11947UKWH00017B/1467